CW01210078

ELEVATION AND BEYOND

A U2 Fan's Travels to Meet the Band, the Crowd, Herself

MARCY GANNON

Emma! (sorry that was a bit shouty)
Dearest Emma,
How blessed I am to have such a coach in you — I had no idea we'd end up here. Thank you, thank you, thank you!
So much love,
Marcy

Elevation and Beyond

© 2021 Marcy Gannon

All rights reserved. No part of this publication may be reproduced, distributed, or transmitted in any form or by any means, including photocopying, recording, or other electronic or mechanical methods, without the prior written permission of the publisher, except in the case of brief quotations embodied in critical reviews and certain other non-commercial uses permitted by copyright law.

ISBN 978-1-66781-655-5

eBook ISBN 978-1-66781-656-2

In loving memory of Billy Bunting, who channeled Bono onstage for nearly 15 years, and never held anything back.

For Elsha, who spent her life demonstrating that anything is possible when love leads the way.

And for my daughter, Julie Grace, who wouldn't be, if it weren't for the music of U2.

The five chapters of this book were written in 2002 or earlier.

CONTENTS

Chapter One:
Out of Isolation 1

Chapter Two:
Elevation 31

Chapter Three:
Revelation 60

Chapter Four:
Separation 97

Chapter Five:
Integration 125

Epilogue:
On to The Miracle 147

A Letter to You from the Author 154

About the Author 158

CHAPTER ONE:
OUT OF ISOLATION

The tiny airplane that was supposed to get me from Chicago's O'Hare airport to Madison, WI made me nervous. I thought to myself, stomach dropping as I gazed out the window, if I'm going to die on this trip, let it be after the U2 shows, please.

On June 24th, 1997, I sat on the plane from O'Hare airport to my first PopMart show. It was the beginning of another dream come true, a fitting follow-up to my year abroad at Trinity College in Dublin Ireland. Time and the world were alive and sparkling. Life was a beautiful thing. These events were once again affirming my faith that life was something I wanted to experience. There had been times over the previous two years in college that I hadn't been so sure of that. Now, on that bumpy flight to Madison for my first U2 show as an adult, I knew that the ghost of depression would not touch me and steal my happiness.

I was just a little kid when I first heard U2 music. The way the singer repeatedly asked, "how long to sing this song?" puzzled me in my concrete, childhood thinking. I wondered logically to myself, "if he wants to stop singing, why doesn't he just stop singing?" Later, at nine years of age, my older brother's room was often full of U2's music and featured a huge poster of the band standing somber and gray in the Arizona desert. At that time, my big brother had a passion for U2 and for the cartoon "Bloom County." Once Chris showed me a joke on the back cover of one of his "Bloom County" books. It was a caricature of U2, with Opus the Penguin posing as The Edge and Bill the Cat as Bono. At nine years old, I didn't quite get the joke. When Mom looked over our shoulders at the cartoon, she said, "Oh, is that BONE-noh?" Fourteen-year-old Chris shook his head and corrected her very uncool pronunciation.

Sometimes, when Chris was away from the house during his increasingly frequent teenage disappearances, I would sneak into his room and gaze upon the big poster of U2 with a child's eyes, feeling somewhat intimidated, even frightened, by their image of stern austerity, and always mesmerized by the angular profile of the lead vocalist.

Vivid childhood snapshots of U2 give way to the haze of growing up. Two days after Christmas 1991, when I was 15 years old, Chris and I were driving along a country road out to my parent's weekend home in rural Virginia, and I fell asleep in the car. I woke up four days later, in the hospital. My mother was sitting in a chair at the foot of my bed. In a weary tone, she told me that Chris and I had been in a car accident. I had staples running up my left hip, and stitches poking out from under my right eye. I had more staples in my knee, closing a puncture wound. I was told that several days had passed since the accident, and during that time I had been in the ICU, where I lay recovering from surgery on my broken left femur and a severe contusion to my brain. This accounted for the half-dozen stitches that sat itching under my eye, and the scary staples bandaged up on my left hip.

When I gingerly went to look in the mirror, I did not recognize the bruised, swollen, and cracked face that stared back at me. I was in a fog.

In the months that followed the accident, I focused on physical recovery and keeping up academically. During the day, I kept my eye on my goals, but in the evening, I was consumed by a profound sense of pain and isolation. I withdrew. I felt insecure socially and began to feel deadened emotionally. A few weeks before the accident, a boy had broken up with me and I had experienced my first encounter with the intense misery of adolescent heartbreak. I took the lesson to mean that I must never allow myself to be vulnerable again. I locked the door to my internal world. The only place that I found an outlet for the bottled up hurt and anger was in writing. I began to write in a journal, discovering that the page was the one thing I trusted with my feelings, which poured out of me in long melodramatic musings and poetry. I stayed in my bedroom with the door closed and wrote through the lonely evenings.

One night, in the spring of 1992, I sat watching VH1 alone in a small room upstairs while the rest of the family gathered around the larger TV downstairs. A video of the song "One" came on. I recognized the singer vaguely as I heard the opening lyrics of the song.

My ears pricked up. The words of the question that opened "One" resonated deeply. I had been asking myself if things were getting better every day since the car accident as I waited for happiness to return to my life. Instead of getting over what had happened (as I understood I should), bitterness was taking root with each day that passed more miserable that the one before.

The song's lyrics continued to present me with words that identified my own deeply buried feelings. To hear someone else name the dark neediness which now characterized my days and nights comforted me. I was mesmerized by the song and by Bono's piercing blue eyes as he sat at a lonely table in a crowded club, smoking a brown cigarette. The words went through me as he seemed to gaze straight out of the cold television and see deep inside me. What a soulful babe! I was hooked on the song and smitten with Bono immediately.

After Mom and Dad went to bed, I ran downstairs and cornered Chris who was out of college for the semester as his broken legs mended. That night I sought to learn from my brother's years as a U2 fan. Chris did the only thing he really could do in response to my curiosity. Chris showed me his video of "Rattle and Hum."

Watching the live concert footage of the late eighties fanned my spark of interest into a flame. Bono's impassioned performances of U2's songs reached in and awoke me from the dark dullness that is depression. Seeing a sexy, shirtless Bono overcome with emotion leave the stage after an intense performance of "Bad" made my eyes glaze over with adolescent infatuation.

"Is Bono married?" I asked Chris.

"Ooh, Marcy's got a crush," taunted big brother before informing me that yes, he was.

The flame was spurred into an inferno.

With the onset of summer 1992, I was fifteen, and freed from academics to make a study of U2. I read Eamon Dunphy's biographical sketch of the band's early history from the 1987 publication The Unforgettable Fire. The fascination continued and grew as I explored everything U2 that I could get my hands on, including their entire back catalogue.

The song "Bad" spoke to me. Chris had told me that it was written about heroin addiction. Though I didn't know much about heroin, the messages of delivery and salvation from a place of blackness were the sort of relief that I needed. Things had gotten worse in my head and darker in my heart as the days passed without any relief from my sense of being lost and alone. Hope for a brighter day spoke to me through the melodies of "Bad."

It was the voice of Bono that spoke such words of hope, and I fell in love with the idea of this man that sang sweet healing messages to me through my headphones and seemed to understand how it felt to be depressed. I could relate to "Bad" more than anything or anyone else in my life. These desolate feelings had taken over my days and nights but stayed locked inside where the heavy energy sat and festered in my heart. "Bad" allowed the negativity to escape and dissipate into the atmosphere for a moment in time. The music was my counselor, teacher, and guru; it led me unfailingly through this therapeutic process.

In June I found out that U2 was in fact on tour and would be coming to Washington D.C.'s RFK stadium in August. Was this a real chance for me to get physically close to this fire? So it seemed. It was not to be missed. The thought of missing it was unacceptable.

My mother hemmed and hawed about letting me go to RFK, and finally agreed only on the condition that I get one of my three older sisters to go with me. I begged and pleaded with Gini, Julie, and Beth until Julie finally caved. I saved my pennies from a job as a clerk in a uniform store and then splurged on two $100 tickets from a ticket broker advertising in the classifieds. I wanted to go to that show, dammit. With tickets in my possession, I sat back and counted the long summer days until August 15, day of show.

Morose and cringing from my parents, I was taken on a family vacation to Colorado in July. I forgot my crankiness as I gazed out the car's backseat window at the wondrous peaks of Rocky Mountain National Park for the first time and listened to the strains of the song "40" pumping through my headphones. I ticked off the days on my calendar excitedly, and nervously, until the concert would arrive.

On the day of the Zoo TV concert, my 30-year-old sister Julie picked me up when she got off work. I was distracted through the afternoon, thinking about an unofficial pre-show meet and greet with the band I might have been missing happening down at the stadium site. Nothing to be done about it at age 15 but wait for my big sister to help me get down there. We took the D.C. Metro Rail down to RFK stadium and fought our way through a crowd of fans to find the seats that my hard-earned dollars had purchased. It was a rainy night and I gazed about me in childlike wonder at the masses of fans filling the stadium. I tried to make sense of the elaborate stage set up. I had never been to an event of this size and felt overwhelmed by the energy and loudness of the stadium. I gazed about with wide eyes at the raucous crowd. I was largely oblivious to the performance of the opening bands. I felt that God himself was about to walk onstage and grace us with His presence.

Therefore, when four human-sized figures came onstage at 10 p.m., it was a bit of a letdown. RFK was so huge, and U2 moved across the mammoth stage, far away and small. The concert itself felt distant and reinforced my feeling of alienation. It confused the hell out of me. Perhaps I went to the show hoping to be healed for good, or even just expecting to see the faces of the men of U2 with my own eyes, but the night was too hazy, and the rain obscured my view of the B-stage, so they remained blurry distant figures from where I stood. Also, they didn't play "Bad"! How could they not play "Bad"? I looked around in dismay as the house lights went up in RFK after two hours of serious rocking, and my sister nudged me, saying it was over. Damn.

They didn't play my favorite song that night, but they did introduce me to the music of ABBA on August 15, 1992. I was less than appreciative.

There was another U2 concert in RFK the next night, but I had no way to get there and no one to take me. I stayed home and listened to the "Concert Playback" on the local radio station. When "Bad" came through my boom box's speakers, I cried and cried.

The summer ended too quickly, and I was soon confronted by the pressures of my junior year in Catholic high school. I started to notice how time slipped by faster and faster, but nothing seemed to change for me emotionally. I had shut down.

I started to rely on U2 music to open me up. I made a couple of mix tapes of select songs that helped me vent anger and feel hope on my blackest days. I would get home from school, after another shitty day, and go out walking, preferably in the rain. I listened to an "Angry U2" mix so that I could get the release of feeling my anger. I did this out of a sense of fear that the depression might squelch the spark of life in me completely. If I could still feel, I could know that I was still alive. "Acrobat" was the first song on the angry mix. The anger in the song seemed to re-ignite the fire that was smoldering in my soul. It voiced my dilemma…I was angry at the world and did not know who to blame but myself. The wail of Edge's guitar solo was the sound of my young mind screaming at a reality I didn't know how to handle, and a future that I feared could only lead to further misery.

To such a stark place came hope, as "Acrobat" ended with words that empowered me to stand up to all the opposition, which I felt always surrounding me, and to keep on dreaming at loud volume, as well as the promise that I could get free of this miserable situation on my own will and strength.

It meant everything to this 15-year-old. After listening to "Acrobat" and other U2 songs of the same mood, I felt strong again, and then I would switch the cassette to a little "Inspirational U2." A song like "Ultraviolet" renewed me energetically. "A Sort of Homecoming" took me to spiritual heights where I escaped to a mythical space beyond pain. It invited me to come away. How wonderful it was! I dreamt of Bono himself coming to me and sweeping me away—I could see the route of escape in my mind; it was a road rising above the horizon and up to the heavens above.

Where organized religion had left me feeling worthless, the vision of the music kept me alive through the blackest of days.

By the end of my junior year in high school, my locker was wallpapered with pictures of the band, and my room was increasingly becoming covered with Bono's mug. I started feeling defensive, then a little freakish, about my growing obsession with the rock group as friends started making cracks and my family observed my behavior with consternation. I didn't want to be odd or un-cool about a band, but I couldn't help it. I had to cling to the hope I found in the music.

I knew I had to get myself away from my unhappy, sheltered Catholic schoolgirl life in Fairfax VA to see some of the world before I went completely insane. I mentioned this ambition for a summer vacation out-of-country to my parents, and they were supportive. My father generously offered to send me to Ireland on a student program for five weeks in the summer of '93. At first, I was put off by the idea of Ireland. That was, like, where my ancestors were from and stuff. Boooooring. But then it occurred to me: U2 lives in Dublin! Maybe I could possibly run into them?

It was decided. I was going.

On July 16, 1993, the day of my scheduled departure from Virginia to join a student group at New York's JFK airport, U2's eighth studio album "Zooropa" was released to the world. I got up at 9 a.m. and drove myself to the local mall, waited outside a record shop until it opened, and picked up the cassette. I drove back home and listened to "Zooropa" for the first time as I finished packing for the trans-Atlantic trip for which I would be leaving in a matter of hours. "Zooropa" was different. It captured my imagination and soothed me, introducing a theme in the title song that stayed with me: the idea that uncertainty could be the very thing that leads us through the darkest times.

That evening, as a plane full of nervously excited 16-year-olds took off from New York for Shannon airport in Western Ireland, I was ready to embrace the uncertainty of the moment and plant some metaphorical flowers of my own.

The five-week stay in Ireland was a wonderful discovery. "Zooropa" pumped through my headset and was soundtrack to my trip as I gazed upon the beautiful gray green mountains of western Ireland from the high schoolers tour bus. A picture of the band hung in my dorm room and watched over me as I fell asleep in my assigned cubicle.

When we got to Dublin for a two week stay, I arrived in the setting of all I had read about U2, and the place where my newfound heroes lived. I felt the magic immediately. I searched for spots that I had read and heard about during my travels through U2-lore over the past year. I took a photo of the Bonavox hearing aid store that was rumored to have been the inspiration for what would become 16-year-old Paul Hewson's lifelong moniker. I had my first cigarette that summer. I tried my first beer too, in the Garage Bar in Dublin, which was owned by U2. As I sipped (excitedly aware of the fact that I was breaking the rules with my underage drinking), I stared in wonder at a Trabant from the Zoo TV tour, mounted and hanging from the ceiling. I met up there with an older, more experienced U2 fan named Amy. She was nineteen and American, and we rode the Dublin Area Rapid Transit out to Killiney, where she said Bono's home was located. It was crazy. What were we doing there? What were we looking for? We both knew Bono and the band were on tour in Europe in support of "Zooropa," and we didn't want to be discovered snooping around his homestead anyway. Or did we?

Craziness continued near the end of the trip, on our last night in Dublin, when I heard that some of my trip mates had been lucky enough to run into The Edge at the Badass Cafe in Temple Bar (the hip, trendy square of the city centre). They showed me the autograph he had given them. I couldn't believe it, and I was green with envy. That night I went into downtown Dublin with the school group to a play at the Abbey Theatre, and once there I snuck out to look for my heroes, now that I knew they were in town today.

I walked. Sixteen, alone, and blissfully independent in this strange and wonderful city, I found my way to Lillie's Bordello on Grafton Street and mentally noted the street crossings and such, hoping to remember how to get back despite the buzz of adrenaline running through my brain. The night was warm, and I felt alive.

Of course, I didn't run into U2, but it was a great night, a fitting end to a great trip. I snuck back into the Abbey Theatre to rejoin the student group undetected, my cheeks flushed from the little adventure. When we flew out of Dublin Airport the next day to begin the trek home, I wept not for having missed out on meeting any members of U2, but for the grief of ending a journey which had drawn me out of the depression that had been over me like a blanket since the accident. The beauty of Ireland had given me new faith in life, and the taste of a new perspective. Ireland drew me into a reality that I felt must be worth living for.

I started my senior year that fall and U2 was placed on my mental back-burner, though their music was constantly pumping through the speakers in my car and my headset. I was miserable to be back home, and the music continued to provide the inspiration that got me through those days of depression. Around the time of finishing my applications for college, the internal pressure got out of hand, and I broke down and asked my mom for help. She took me to a doctor who told me there was a chemical imbalance in my brain, and prescribed Prozac. At the time, I had some misgivings about going on medication for a mental condition that seemed to reflect weakness, but I was so sick of myself and my life by then that I just didn't care. I accepted the drugs with relief and hoped they would work.

They did. Within about two weeks the cloud of anxiety and hopelessness hanging over my head had dissolved considerably. I looked forward to the future with a zest I hadn't felt in three years. I felt sad that I had lost so much time and resolved to live my life to the fullest from there on out. The end of a lousy four years was celebrated at high school commencement in

1994. I chose a university situated in the beautiful Shenandoah Valley of the Blue Ridge Mountains in rural Virginia and made a promise to myself to go study in Dublin Ireland during my third year in college.

In the spring of '96 I received word that I had been accepted to a study abroad program at Trinity College. Joy! I would soon return to that mystical place that had felt so like home when I had visited three years ago. Behind this, still in the back of my mind sat the hopeful possibility of running into Bono or Edge on the street just once over the course of an entire academic year in Dublin.

What a year it was. Swept up in an American student's life at Trinity College Dublin, I mostly forgot about Bono and Edge and Adam and Larry. Until it became known that the band's next studio album, the first in four years, would be released in March of 1997. I harbored wishful-thinking sorts of ideas that perhaps the band would come out on release night in their own hometown and check out the scene at the local retailer (as they once had in the past). Leaving our local pub at 11 p.m. and catching the 15 Bus north into the city, my roommate Erin and I went down to HMV on Grafton Street for a midnight release party. It was quite a scene, filled with Irish fans that had come out from the pubs for this midnight sale and were rabid for more U2. But there was no sign of Bono.

Following my mild disappointment in not encountering the band (again), Erin and I returned to the student flat where we were staying in Rathmines, a small suburban area just south of City Centre. We listened to the new CD, called "Pop," until the wee hours of the morning. For the final three months of my student year in Dublin, "Pop" played continuously through my headset.

Although "Pop" would receive a lukewarm reception in the US, I loved the CD. As young as I was, I was free of expectations about U2 that came from what they had done in the eighties. The spirit of the music was still audible through the distortion and techno rhythms that some of their old-school fans in the US had a hard time accepting. The soul of the music called out to me clearly, layered over the funky growling beat, especially on songs like "Mofo" and "Do You Feel Loved." I heard the rocking U2 that older fans seemed to be longing for on the tracks "Last Night on Earth" and "Gone." The new technology added a layer of incredible colors and moods to the mix. This sort of moodiness made the song "If You Wear That Velvet Dress" the sexiest U2 song to date.

I never did run into any members of the band during that academic year in Dublin. Still, it was a lively nine months. Unfortunately, that same nine months spanned over the first three months of U2's PopMart tour, including the date that they were scheduled to play Washington, DC. I was distraught when I caught wind of their tour dates and discovered that the week they would be in DC, I would begin writing for exams at Trinity. I shared my conundrum with my father. To my surprise and delight he helped me figure out a plan so that I could travel to visit family in the Midwest following my return from Dublin, to coincide with the tour schedule. I would catch a show on my own in Madison WI, staying with my aunt who lived there, then meet my brother Chris in Chicago for the show two nights later at Soldier Field. My American flat mates in Ireland, Erin and Erica, wanted to see a show on the PopMart tour too, and we hatched a plan to meet up for a show in Boston in July. With this small itinerary in mind, I ordered six tickets to three PopMart shows from Propaganda, the official fan magazine, to which I had subscribed back in 1992 for the sole purpose of future ticket procurement. The future had arrived, and I was very excited.

In fact, the excitement of my impending minitour blunted the pain of leaving Ireland again. Following my return from Trinity in mid-June I had only two weeks to kill in my parents' home before I would board a plane to Madison, WI for the first of three planned PopMart shows.

When I arrived in Madison, at the home of my Aunt Patricia, I was thrilled to find that she lived a short walking distance from Camp Randall Stadium, where the golden arches of PopMart stood tall and were visible from outside, peaking above the upper decks.

The next morning, after a night of endless conversation, coffee, and cigarettes with my wonderful 70-year-old aunt, I was greeted by a bright hot summer day. As I walked to the stadium, I took in the scene around me with fascination. I rounded the bend from Aunt Pat's house, passing scalpers and fans as I got closer, seeking the Golden Arch of the PopMart stage. There was nowhere else in the world, or in my mind, that I would rather be that afternoon. Nowhere.

Having read stories of fan-band encounters via Internet fan groups, I sought the entrance that U2 might drive through within hours. I found fellow diehard fans there and I joined them in their wait. There was a good crowd, and I struck up a conversation with a girl sitting in the grass near me. We chatted and waited as other fans moved about with U2 collectibles they hoped to have autographed and sat near us on the grass and greeted each other. There was anticipation in the hot summer air, and the heat of the day matched the redness of my legs, which were sunburned lobster red from a foolish day of basking in the hot summer sun earlier in the week. My father had poked his head out the door onto the deck that day and said to me, "Two words: SKIN CANCER." Of course, I hadn't listened. Luckily the pain of my sunburn couldn't pierce through the sense of wonder and joyful anticipation that hung about the day.

We sat and stood together and waited, like children waiting for Santa Claus. We waited impatient and driven, with hopes of seeing the band members up close, and in the flesh, to have proof of their existence, their realness, more concrete than the dim view from far off stage or the synthetic chill of the television. We waited for hours, then after waiting through soundcheck, my restlessness overcame me. I gave up and took off for a bite to eat at Aunt Pat's before the show. Upon return to the stadium,

I learned that U2 had arrived, but were now elusively concealed in the nether regions of backstage.

There was a buzz about me, and about the stadium, as I found my seat in the first tier off Adam's side of the stage. This was a great seat, courtesy of Propaganda. I clutched my program impatiently: I had never waited so long for anything in my life! Still, I would have been willing to wait through any number of hours more for the promise of the band's arrival. I was by myself, yet un-self-conscious and lost in my own world; what I began to think of as my own U2opia. There were friendly lads seated next to me who seemed to think I was cool as opposed to crazy. I sat happily in my solitude because I didn't feel alone. My most faithful companion of the last five years was there with me, in the form of U2's music. The four men who made it would soon be out to shower their musical bliss upon all of us thousands congregated there.

I was intoxicated by this perfect reality as I watched the lights of the stadium finally dim and the PopMart Globe logo came up onscreen. "Pop Musik" that old M song I had never heard before, pumped through the speakers, and the crowd rose to its feet to greet for unimposing man from Dublin.

And then, of course, there they were, and the next two hours were dripping with magic. My heart breathed a sigh of relief after five years of waiting, waiting, for my next shot to go to a U2 concert and make it better for myself this time. I had been waiting to make a memory. I was relieved to finally make up for that lost chance I had in 1992 at the Zoo TV show, when I had been too young to really understand.

During "One," as the show wrapped up that night, I took off for the outside gates of the backstage area, hoping to have a closer glimpse at the band, hoping they may have a glimpse of me as their motorcade—"four jerks in a police escort"—would pull away and make off for the night. Momentarily, after the strains of "I Can't Help Falling in Love With You" finished echoing out of the stadium and into the warm Wisconsin night, we saw the motorcade coming. Here was Adam, sitting and looking ahead in the first car, and Edge, smiling and waving out at us from the second car—*he sees me!* I thought to myself. A woman cried out from the ranks of those gathered, "Show us your face, Bono!" But alas, it was not to be. Our favorite man stayed hidden and protected from the endlessly adoring eyes tonight.

I walked back to Aunt Pat's feeling completely overwhelmed with pleasure. The concert had blown my mind and filled up my heart with love. This mantra ran through my satisfied soul: SO MUCH BETTER THAN SEX!

Two days later I hugged Patricia goodbye and hopped back on the bus heading south to O'Hare airport, where my brother was scheduled to pick me up for the show in Chicago on June 27th. That evening Chris and I entered Soldier Field together. Joy coursed through my veins as it had for the past several days. Looking at the Propaganda tickets before the show, we noted that they said Section B Row 9. As we entered with the crowds of fans that now converged upon Soldier Field, I figured our seats were in the reserved seating section along a tier to the side of the stage. I was wrong. It wasn't until we were continually waved through by security and found our assigned seats on the field in the 9th row that reality hit me. Reality appeared to be 9th row, center field seats, at a stadium U2 concert? It was the stuff my dreams were made of. Chris turned to look at the massive structure around us and behind us. He nudged me, laughing, "There are people *way back there,* man!" He directed my gaze to the nosebleed sections of Soldier Field. I remained speechless as his excitement turned into laughter. Chris, being the original U2 fan, was possibly just as excited as I was to find us there. We had been waved forward past security checkpoint after security checkpoint, until it felt like we were about thirty feet from Larry's drum kit in this gigantic house.

Well, I was given an inch and I took a mile. I grabbed my big brother and we set off for the railing along the side of the catwalk that stretched well out into the audience. I tried to pick a spot that seemed to resemble a place where Bono had chosen the girl to join him on stage in Madison. I couldn't believe that this rock star that had turned into a mythical hero for me would be performing mere feet away from us before the night was over. I chatted happily with fans I had met two days ago in Wisconsin, and we waited for the show to get going again.

Soon, we were swept into another amazing show. It was such a thrill to see the band up close and in the flesh, with a completely unimpeded view during certain parts of the show. I watched Bono and Edge perform their mock matador routine during "Until the End of The World" right in front of us, just as I had watched it on my video player so many times over the past five years. We partied. When the massive mirror ball lemon moved out across the catwalk toward the B-stage, its parking location turned out to be directly above us. The shining pod was a giant colossus from this angle. Swirling streams of starry light swished through the smoky air, pounding to the pulsing beat of the "Lemon" remix. I danced and lifted my arms as Bono swaggered before us, checking out those of us along the rail during "Mysterious Ways." I screamed my hellos to him with everybody else.

As the concert ended, it would be goodbye to the fans and the shows for a few days. Bono's sweet Hallelujah chorus was added to the end of "One" that night, and precisely voiced my feelings about the evening.

Following a weekend back home with the family in Virginia, I caught another plane to Boston, where I met up with Erin and Erica. It was a joyful reunion between the three of us, though we had only been away from each other for about a month. We spent time at an Irish pub and drank pints of Guinness before heading to the stadium outside of Boston for the show. We spent more time in the parking lot tailgating, and before I knew it, I was unable to go on because I had had too much to drink. I was lying in the backseat of Erica's car, moaning, when my friends said they were so sorry to leave me, but it was time to head in. I still couldn't go. They left me with my ticket, and I lay there, crying as I heard the show starting.

When the chords of "New Year's Day" rang out into the night air, I found the will to stumble inside. I took my floor ticket and found my way down into a crush of bodies near the B-stage. Eventually, in my weakened state, the crush was too much for me, and I moved out of the crowd to take in the final encore from a distance. Bono added the lines of "MLK" to the conclusion of "One" that night.

The soothing lullaby was a balm to my heart's mourning. This night marked the end of the joyful experience that three U2 concerts in one week had been. It had happened far too fast. I was sad and wanted more. My appetite for U2 remained insatiable.

In the fall, the band returned to the US on the third leg of the PopMart tour, and I traveled to the U2 show in St. Louis on November 8, the eve of my 21st birthday with my excellent friend Cate. She had a brother conveniently located in St. Louis with whom we could crash following the long car ride from Virginia. I decided to go all out in a bid for Bono's attention, in hopes of getting onstage for a dance.

I got this idea back in the springtime before the tour that I could take the suggestion of "If You Wear That Velvet Dress" literally. I could go ahead and wear a velvet dress to a PopMart show to try and catch Bono's eye. I didn't have the guts to do it in the summer, but now, after having experienced three nights of PopMart, I was ready to take a risk. What the hell, I figured, what's the worst thing that can happen to me? Disappointment and humiliation? Who cares? I didn't. I was still in love with that idealized vision of Bono that had taken root in my adolescent mind five years prior. I wanted to meet him, and I most definitely wanted the chance to give him a very big hug. It was worth the risk.

I went out and bought a little velvet dress for twenty dollars at TJ Maxx and a long-sleeved silver jacket to wear over the short, sleeveless dress (after all, this would be November in St. Louis). The outfit seemed to fit well with all the glitter and disco and whatnot of this tour. I colored a poster announcing to Bono himself that it was my 21st birthday and I was wearing "that velvet dress" so PLEASE dance with me! It was lovely, covered with bright lettering and glitter.

I felt that there was no way that this could really happen, even as I did what I could to make it happen. No way could life be this kind. I was nervous as hell when we entered the TransWorld Dome in St. Louis, and more than a little stoned from a joint we had smoked pre-show in the car. I was with Erin, my friend from Ireland whom I had last seen at the time of the Boston show several months prior. Erin had traveled from her home in Kansas City to meet Cate and I for the show. I got even more wound up as we managed to stake a claim along the B-stage fence, and I realized that chances were damn good that Bono would spot me and my sign.

The show itself killed my anxiety, which was boiling over by the time it got started. I got lost in the music, and I lost the complete preoccupation with the idea of a dance with Bono. It was so wonderful to be back at a U2 concert with my friend Erin standing next to me, and at times with the band members just a few feet in front of us on the B-stage. Surprisingly, the TransWorld Dome was only about half full. We couldn't have cared less, us PopMartians down around the B-stage. The party continued.

As the first encore began, the full band descended from the lemon and performed from the B-stage. For a long moment, the spotlight shone on Bono and spilled across the stage beyond him and onto me. It lit up my sparkling poster. I thought to myself, "this could be it." To my profound delight, Bono turned, walked over, and stopped at the edge of the stage in front of me. He looked down at me and deliberately read my poster as his toe kept tapping to the beat. This took a fair few seconds, because the sign was rather wordy (it had been a concern of a good friend of mine that

Bono wouldn't have the time or interest to catch the gist of it). While he was there, I blew him a kiss. He smiled flirtily, knowingly at me, and turned around back to the band to continue singing "Discotheque." The words to the bridge of "Discotheque" that he sang in that moment were eerily appropriate to the situation. I felt something big happening tonight.

The momentary connection with Bono as he read my sign and smirked at me was incredibly satisfying. In fact, the fans around me patted me on the shoulder in congratulations. I thought that could be the end of it, and it was more than adequate to please me. I mean, I had communicated with Bono…what else can a fan ask for other than the opportunity for a meeting of the eyes with their chosen idol?

But, as it turned out, that was only the beginning. Bono came back and stood before me after "Discotheque" ended, as the band segued into "Velvet Dress." Before I realized what was happening, the man was beckoning for me to join him up onstage. *Who, me?* My hand fluttered to my chest in a wide-eyed sort of innocent, humble gesture. In response, Bono nodded and beckoned me with another crook of his finger as he softly chanted "come up, come up" into the microphone.

I really couldn't believe this, but I didn't waste any time thinking about it. Instead, I dropped my poster which I had been tightly clutching against the railing throughout the entire show, onto the floor like a rock. I made my way through the crowd along the rail, thinking I would be allowed onstage through the B-stage gate that the band had entered by at the show's start. When I got there, I felt myself being lifted over the fence by my fellow fans. I made it over the fence, completely banging and bruising my shins in the process, although I felt no pain at that point.

Once I was inside the fence, between the crowd and the stage, a giant security man looked down at me. He said, looking surprised and angry, "What do you think you're doing??" I blinked and pointed up at Bono who stood just a few feet away at the top of the stairs, watching me from behind Giant's back. "He's—he's waiting for me!!" I stuttered. Giant Security Man looked up and saw Bono watching this interchange, then stepped aside to let me pass. I climbed the stairs and took Bono's outstretched hand, placing my other hand on his shoulder. I was grinning mightily and shaking my head slightly in disbelief as I gazed at him, as the opening chords of "Velvet Dress" lingered in the air.

Bono did something then that I didn't really understand. He removed my purse from across my body and set it on the stage behind him. He turned back to me and gently pushed my silver jacket off my bare shoulders, then removed my jacket completely. My jaw dropped and I laughed a bit in shock as I awkwardly tried to help. Then, happily, I allowed myself to be pulled close to him for a slow dance.

I was pulled into heaven. My ability to think was gone as I found myself wrapped in a very real, very tight embrace with this symbolic figure of love and masculinity in my psyche. I couldn't believe how small Bono was, how good he smelled despite the sweat glistening on his scalp, and how much he felt just like other men that I had held before. We swayed and circled slowly under the spinning lights of the disco ball lemon. When the song ended, Bono guided me back towards the stairs and I was ready to leave the stage, but he grasped my shoulder firmly and pulled me down to sit with him on the stairs as "With or Without You" began. My insides lit up and my jaw dropped into an open-mouthed grin as I realized I could stay with him a little while longer. I turned my gaze back to where Erin was against the railing and locked eyes with her in amazement. She was there, grinning hugely for me, as I turned back to him and relaxed, laying my head on his shoulder. I closed my eyes and forgot the presence of 30,000 concert attendees watching this show. I smiled as I felt him gently stroking my hair, then may have fallen into a brief faint as I leaned against him.

When I opened my eyes, I was startled by my direct view down into the man's lap. I looked up immediately from Bono's pelvic region, only to be startled again at the sight of dozens of faces shining before me, and a cameraman filming us a few feet away at the bottom of the stairs. Soon enough, Bono pulled away to stand up. I looked through his shades into those piercing blues one last time, then departed the stage.

Whew! I clumsily stumbled over the fence, through the fans, and back to my spot next to Erin. We embraced, and I stood in a total daze as fans nearby patted me on the back and grinned at me. I still couldn't think. I was completely overwhelmed and incredulous about what had just happened and could barely process the incoming stimuli. "With Or Without You" ended with the beloved and rarely heard "Shine Like Stars" coda, and the band waved their thank yous as they departed the B-stage. I heard Bono thanking the opening band, Third Eye Blind, and then he effected an Elvis like drawl and said quietly "thanks for the dance, that was…that was very Elvis of you."

I was still far gone when the band returned for the final encore. It was the sight of the giant red heart filling the PopMart screen as "One" neared its conclusion that woke me from my shocked reverie. The image seemed to be that of my own heart, projecting onto the screen as it overflowed with wonder and joy, and above all: love. Love for the music, and love for the experience of a U2 concert, and love for life itself.

In the months following the St. Louis show, I was distracted much of the time, constantly reliving this incredible dream come true. I thought about the dance with Bono a great deal, and I fell into a funk over the end of the North American tour. After St. Louis, the song "Do You Feel Loved" took on a whole new meaning. Hell, yeah, I had felt loved! The seeds of an ambitious plan to follow the band through the US much more closely on their next tour had been planted and were germinating in my mind.

The final PopMart show on this side of the Atlantic was broadcast live from Mexico City on December 2, 1997 and aired on pay-per-view in the US. Bono said thanks to the PopMartians at the end of the show, and the online community from which the name had sprung rejoiced at the public acknowledgement. There was a period of recovery from this tour, and the internet mailing list group called Wire talked about concert withdrawal. I took comfort there until life swept me away from the computer screen and onto college graduation in the spring of 1998.

All signs pointed to a need to find direction, a mission for my life. I didn't know what I wanted to do after college graduation, so I did the only thing that seemed to make sense. I readied myself to return to Ireland for another four months of living, allowed to be there this time on a student work visa.

It was good to be back in Dublin when I arrived in May of 1998. I looked forward to four months of quiet living and working in this beloved city that had for the past five years been the symbol of a spiritual home in my mind in my heart. Still on that back burner sat the idea that maybe this time I could possibly run into U2. Although I didn't really know if I wanted to, after the ideal fantasy-reality experience I had enjoyed in St. Louis on November 8th of last year. It seemed I would be destined for disillusionment if I did finally have that more mundane experience of running into one of the band members in Dublin. Still, I couldn't help but feel curious as to whether Bono or even Edge might possibly remember the velvet dress girl from St. Louis.

Life plugged along with work and socializing with Irish friends from my year at Trinity. One afternoon in July, we were at the Octagon Bar, a part of the Clarence Hotel in Temple Bar. The Clarence was owned by U2. We had often partied at the affiliated nightclub downstairs called The Kitchen, but we had never been in the Octagon. We had a gang of about six friends drinking pints and looking at the wealthy types that seemed more suited to be at this ritzy hotel than us. My Irish friends had agreed to go there with me as a concession to my tenacious curiosity around all things U2. We'd been there for several hours and were well on our way to drunkenness when my friend Astrid asked to borrow my mobile to call a mutual friend and see if he could join us. After a few moments, I followed Astrid into the hallway that led to the lobby of the Clarence, to annoy her as she spoke with our friend over the phone. My head swiveled from Ast, and my jaw dropped as I observed Edge walking into the lobby in the company of about three people. Astrid quipped to our friend Gareth that The Edge had just entered the building and Marcy was about to start hyperventilating. Instinctively, I moved towards the lobby as Edge's entourage moved into the other room and the guitarist stood solo at the hotel desk talking with the clerk there.

After he broke from the conversation with the clerk, I approached The Edge and nervously introduced myself, explaining in a rush that I had been a fan for years and that I had gone to see four PopMart shows and then I had been pulled on stage in St. Louis, but I didn't suppose he remembered me...? Edge looked at me quizzically and asked me my name again, then very kindly shook my hand and told me he was glad I had enjoyed their shows. The Edge then bid me adieu and joined his friends in the room into which they had disappeared only moments before he had been approached by this tipsy, eager, and perhaps slightly scary fan.

I turned, feeling rather silly, and went back into the Octagon Bar. Seeing my face, Astrid said to Gareth on the other end of the phone "Uh oh, looks like that didn't go well." I sat down in the bar with my friends, and we discussed the incident. Later, Edge popped into the bar in the company of his friends. Feeling embarrassed by my forwardness earlier, I tried to disappear into a dark corner of our table then forced myself not to stare at the cowboy hatted guitar hero. Edge stood there in the entrance to the bar for only a moment then disappeared back into the hallway with his companions.

It had indeed been rather anti-climactic. Still, part of me was pleased that the encounter in Dublin had finally happened.

A few weeks later, I caught word online that the band was at work on new material in Hanover Quay Studios, which was located just across the River Liffey from where I was working as a receptionist in a gas supply company. This news caught my attention. I had read many stories of fans meeting and chatting with the band rather casually by hanging out and waiting for them to emerge from their recording studios. Impulsively, after work the very next day, I caught a bus to City Centre and met Astrid, who was kind enough to agree to walk down to the studios with me for moral support.

After a pint or two at a local pub, we set out for Hanover Quay. I carried with me a plastic folder containing a four-page essay I had written about my personal PopMart tour. I hoped to give it to Bono.

It was a damp evening and at about 6:00 p.m. the sun was setting over the Docklands of Dublin. We strolled casually down to the studio, which stood humbly amidst concrete surroundings. There was an old trailer and a trash fire in the alley round the corner where a homeless man warmed his hands. When we rounded the corner to Hanover Quay, my body buzzed with excitement as I noticed that there were five cars lining the curb in front of the studio. As soon as I saw the vehicles, I knew U2 was inside. I told Astrid, "They're here!"

We waited a bit, and the anticipation was killing me. It started growing colder as the sun sank in the grey, dripping sky. I clutched my plastic folder to my chest and waited some more, hoping Astrid wouldn't give up on the situation before the band would come out. We entertained ourselves by playing match the car with its U2 owner (guesswork really). Luckily, before too long we got some action. The handle turned on the large steel door on the front of the studio. A man with close cut grey hair, white-rimmed glasses, and a cigarette hanging out of his mouth stepped outside.

"That's Adam!" I said to Astrid in a sideways whisper.

"Yes, it is," she replied in a normal tone.

"Hi Adam!" I called out cheerfully, determined to be a little bit more normal than I had been in The Clarence, chattering at The Edge.

"How's it going?" replied Adam, smiling at us around his smoke as he opened the door to his small blue car.

"Working hard in there?" quipped Astrid. Adam smiled and nodded and drove out to the main road.

Mere moments later, the studio door handle turned again. I dropped the cigarette that I was smoking, post Adam encounter, onto the concrete sidewalk. Larry, in his insane gorgeousness, walked out of the studio.

"That's Larry!" I whispered brilliantly to Astrid.

"It sure is," she agreed.

"Hi, Larry!" I called out amicably, ever so cheerful and calm.

Larry looked over at us, smirking. He replied, "Howyeh," then climbed into his car and took off down the alley. Astrid and I were both immediately reduced to giggling, starstruck girls. I'm sure this was some sort of female chemical response automatically triggered when a super-hot, non-aging James Dean looking member of the rock star species comes into view. Purely chemical.

Well, after that burst of excitement, there was more waiting to be done. It was getting cold and wet, and we shivered and huddled under a small umbrella. It got turned inside out over our heads by cold gusts of wind. Astrid began making noises about going to meet her twin for pints as scheduled. I told her she could go, but I was going nowhere. I was not budging. Finally, after about another hour or so in the darkening night, the rain let up. The door handle turned again.

Up next for fan meet and greet, please welcome…The Edge! Rays of light filtered out onto the cold cobblestone alley from the large front door, which Edge left open behind him.

I chirped, "Hi, Edge!"

Edge looked up and turned toward us, saying, "I'm sorry I can't stay long, I'm already late."

More than a little flustered, I fumbled in my plastic folder and said, "Well I have something here to give Bono," but before I could find it Edge replied, "Oh, he'll be out in a minute." What? Edge just told me what? Is this for real? I thought to myself.

Stupidly, I started to mention to Edge that I had met him a few weeks earlier at his hotel. Luckily, Astrid piped up and interrupted me. She shared with him that I had been pulled on stage in St. Louis, and he said that he knew I looked familiar from somewhere (yes perhaps from your hotel's lobby a few weeks ago, but on second thought we won't mention that one, will we?).

Embarrassed, I mentioned something about a velvet dress, and how it had worked for me, and Edge interjected in a sincere voice, "Yeah! It worked great." I said to him, surprised, "You remember that?" He assured me that he remembered it and called it "a great moment." Wow. It was super cool of him to say that, even if he was just being kind, and had no idea what we were on about.

Edge was very kind, despite his rush. My nervousness was replaced by a sort of heightened sense of reality, tinged with pleasure at Edge's generosity. He kindly agreed to pose for a photo with me. "That's the easy part," he said. Handshakes went around and Edge went on his way in his beautiful silver Mercedes. Our attention moved back to the still open door to the studio, and the warm, well-lit place within.

A short, dark figure emerged almost immediately (it's as if they had planned it…one at a time, don't overexcite the females out front now, lads). Bono stepped right out and came towards us.

I called out, "Bono, can I give you something?" This seemed like a good icebreaker. Sure, it was better than my opener with Edge.

"Sure," Bono replied as he crossed the alley between us.

I gave him my essay, now glad that I had rather self-consciously penned a note directly to the rock star on the back that afternoon. I passed the pages to him, explaining that this was some writing I had done on the PopMart shows I had attended. I inwardly cringed as he folded up the carefully preserved sheets and stuck the essay in his back pocket. Ah well.

I told him that I had been lucky enough to see four PopMart concerts, and that I had had the chance to see the show both from right up close and far up in the stands. He put on a Rastafarian accent, referring to the folks who liked to get high and watch the show from far away, and it made me and Astrid laugh. I had to keep checking myself, almost mentally pinching myself, thinking I'd wake up and find I had passed through a doorway to some alternate reality. It was simply unbelievable to be talking with him after all these years as a super fan. When I told him he danced with me in St. Louis, he just looked at me blankly. I mentioned that I had been wearing a velvet dress, and he remarked, "Yes, well that would do it."

He was very kind, and warm, and his eyes were only partially obscured by lightly tinted shades. His hair was growing out from the buzz cut he wore on the PopMart tour, and I was glad. He posed with me for a picture, grabbing me and pulling me close with his cheek pressed against mine. To my distress, the camera made sputtering noises as Astrid tried to get the photo. He said, "Well let's try again," and patiently waited as she tried again to no avail. I genuinely didn't want to inconvenience him, so I said, ah that's alright.

Then Bono turned and shook our hands. Looking directly into my eyes one more time, he bowed before me and kissed the back of mine, then turned to go on his way, crossing the alley towards his car. We watched him, shivering woefully. I went for it and said, "I don't suppose we could catch a lift into town, could we?" He turned back and asked where we were headed. Since we were meeting up with friends after this, I answered literally, blurting out "Temple Bar." At the same time, Astrid saved the day again, brilliantly quipping, "*Wherever!*"

In response, Bono kindly offered to "get us as close to Temple Bar" as he could, and said he would pull the car out from the curb so we could get in.

Incredible! We looked wide-eyed at each other as Bono moved the car, and then hopped out, opening the doors for us. Astrid told me to take shotgun, and I did. I found myself getting comfortable on a cowhide seat in Bono's stylish yellow Mercedes as he closed the door behind me. This is crazy! I thought to myself as I tried to recall how to buckle a seatbelt. It was quite a task in this excited state.

As soon as Bono took his seat behind the wheel, I immediately went into inquisitive mode.

"I hear that you are working on a 'Best of the Eighties' compilation in there, is that right?" I asked him.

Bono ignored my question and instead began to apologize for the smell inside the vehicle… "Sorry it smells like cow shit in here!" he exclaimed, laughing. "I got these cowhide seats, and they stink!"

It didn't smell remotely like cow shit in Bono's car. Astrid said from the back seat, "Ah sure don't worry, my car smells like cat piss!" and they were both laughing.

What does my car smell like, I thought desperately to myself? Cigarette smoke? But that's not funny. I said nothing.

Bono continued, "I picked up these cowhide seats while I was going through my Cuban Dictator phase."

I cracked, "Yeah, well, we all go through that." Astrid laughed, but Bono didn't!

Instead of giving a chuckle out of respect for my great sense of humor, Bono went into a story about a homeless man he once came across who stood around on the street muttering to himself, "fuck the gardai, fuck the gardai" until the garda came into view and then he changed his tune to "Up the gardai! Up the gardai!" Bono enjoyed his story, laughing away. I was confused, wondering if he might answer my question yet, or if it had been a mistake to ask questions at all.

Then, he did! He said yes, they were working on the eighties compilation, and he was most enthusiastic about a compilation of B-sides that they were putting together. I interjected then, sharing that I used to have a B-sides compilation cassette of my own, but it was rather overworn and could use a replacement. He shared that they were working on the old track "The Sweetest Thing" and he was pleased with the remake they were coming up with. I interrupted again, saying, "That's a great song! Totally underrated!"

He seemed to get excited then, and began rummaging around in the space between our front seats, saying, "Oh great I will play it for you, I have it here somewhere…"

He kept rummaging while trying to drive through the dark wet Dublin night, as Astrid said, "that must be really cool, to go back and work on something that you did a long time ago."

I was beginning to get nervous about the driving as he continued to search for the cassette to no avail, and I said "Ah that's ok, we can hear it on the radio with everyone else."

Bono gave up the search and kept chatting in response to Astrid's comment as I (not so) subtly stared at his profile. I recognized the freckles speckled across his left cheek from all the videos and photos I had stared at over the years, and I felt the strangest sensation in my body. As if my whole body was being squeezed through the top of my head and out into space. It was extraordinarily bizarre to be riding shotgun in Bono's car while he drove us through Dublin, and the energy flows in my body were responding in dramatic fashion!

I noticed that we were rounding the corner to Trinity College then, and not wanting to inconvenience him any further, I politely and stupidly told our unlikely driver that we could hop out here. He pulled over, and after making sure we knew where we were going, he sped off into the gloomy Dublin night. Astrid and I stood on the curbside, giggling, and holding hands, and almost getting run over by oncoming traffic as we watched Bono drive away.

Of course, I have no idea whether Bono read my essay or not. It doesn't really matter. That I was able to give it to him was another incredible, fan faith affirming experience, and it made it easier to move beyond memories of the onstage dance we had in St. Louis. It was some sort of closure. It brought home the reality that Bono was a real human who puts his pants on one leg at a time, can't find a cassette tape when he wants it, and keeps talking even when I want to say something. After that night, I knew I was ready to go home to face my future, while saving my pennies for a time that would bring the band back to the US. It would happen with the Elevation Tour in 2001.

CHAPTER TWO:
ELEVATION

In the fall of 2000, the news came. The new album was coming in October. *Here we go,* I thought to myself. Time to hope back on the U2 train. With the release of "Beautiful Day," anticipation for the new record increased. When album release day rolled around, I took an hour off work in the middle of the day and drove through the Virginia countryside, taking in my first impression of "All That You Can't Leave Behind."

It was an optimistic chunk of music, and I enjoyed it, but I found it rather simplistic lyrically and I was disappointed that it wasn't full of hard rocking tracks. "Elevation" was a notable exception, and it was my immediate favorite.

Despite my initial mild disappointment with the latest release, I kept my eyes and ears open for tour news. Obviously, the tour would be starting in the spring of 2001. I would be ready.

What I was *not* ready for was the surprise announcement that U2 would be doing a gig at a nightclub in New York on December 5th. Nor was I prepared for the subsequent radio giveaway, which was the only way to get tickets to the dream gig. I went to extraordinary efforts, including a rather embarrassing incident where I showed up at the local radio station in a velvet dress to beg the DJ on-air for a pair of tickets. I found myself ticket-less at show time, and happy enough to sit at home with a glass of wine to listen to the show broadcast live over the radio.

It was so cool to hear the first show on American soil in over three years through the radio as it happened. I did not know the Ramones song that Bono sang, but I liked it. I did not know what he was doing with the whole "introducing the band" bit, but it made me laugh. When they played "Bad," I just didn't know what hit me. Tears began to flow spontaneously as I realized I would likely finally get to see them perform my favorite song in concert for the first time in the not-too-distant future. After this broadcast, the excitement and anticipation of seeing U2 again took over. I was hurled into a state of mad enthusiasm.

In mid-December, rumors began flowing online of supposed tour dates. I joined a News Group of fans talking tour plans through U2tours.com. We dreamed of the impending tour together as we waited for the official word. During this time frame I considered the problem of ticket procurement. The word online was that Propaganda would be offering fewer tickets for mail order per member this time around. Since I would be going to more shows than I had last time, I chose to set up a safety net to ensure that I would get all the tickets necessary to see this eight-year-old idea come to fruition. I buried a minor amount of guilt about the manipulative nature of the action and signed up several friends and family members to

Propaganda before the tour dates were announced, so I could use their ticket order forms. The weight of my ambition easily beat out any ethical misgivings I harbored.

The stage was set for a super flurry of planning activity when the official dates were announced in mid-January. I spent the next week figuring out a plausible tour route. I soon found myself on MapQuest plotting driving routes from DC: south to Atlanta, west to Chicago, and north to Boston.

For now, it looked like I would be joining the tour in the American cities of Charlotte, Atlanta, Pittsburgh, Columbus, Indianapolis, Chicago, Albany, Hartford, Boston, and Philly. I was determined to run for a while with the tour this time, and once the Prop order forms started arriving, I found myself emptying out my savings account as I sent money orders for hundreds of dollars into their ticketing company. I said a silent prayer as I dropped my savings written across 7-Eleven money orders into the irretrievable depths of the mail slot.

During the second half of January, I began drawing up spreadsheets of expense estimates, days needed off, and mileage anticipated. I spent evenings after work canoodling around with a map of the United States, drawing out routes planned from city to city and marking off lodging plans, all color coordinated, divided into three separate legs of the journey. The first Saturday the Elevation shows went on sale I was at my boyfriend Ro's house in Annapolis. He was amazingly supportive about the whole crazy scheme. After scoring the four tickets I needed to the Chicago show, I crashed out. It had been a busy week.

I whiled away long hours at work in February reading Internet postings from other U2-heads busting at the seams with excitement and comparing tour plans. It was through the sharing of ideas and endless Internet communique that the idea to create a belly dancer costume was born. I bought fabric, jewelry, and makeup, and planned to get all geared up at the Atlanta show on March 30th. Chuckling madly to myself as I studied the "Mysterious Ways" video, I would sit and stitch shiny gold fabric, bells, fringe, and other doodads onto a red satin bra which would double as my belly dancer top. I had to admit to myself that I had designs on perhaps getting Bono's attention, and giving him his very own personal belly dance, but I told myself that my main motivations for doing this were just to have a great time and get into the spirit.

I created a fan signature book with a question on the cover, "What makes YOU elevate?" to pass around to the good people on their way to finding new heights with me in the GA line for the shows. I watched U2 pull a move like the decision to use general admission on the floor, and to return to the arenas, and worried that they were finally selling out for real. It all seemed to be a rather obvious strategy to get back into the superstar spotlight, which had faded a bit from them in the States with the PopMart Tour. I worried that their voice would be compromised by commercialism as so many others had been. But I didn't worry too much. Mostly I just got more and more excited as I once again ticked off the days on my calendar nearing March 29th, the day of the show in Charlotte, which would be my first.

On March 22nd I wrote in my pre-tour journal:

I feel like a little kid at Christmas! It's really a great feeling though. It's why I do this anyway. It's feeling alive again, feeling magic come back into your life. The start of spring brings awakenings of all kinds, and I'm lucky that the experience of U2 live is going to be reborn with this season this year. Because it's going to be such an adventure. And I just love an adventure.

I passed the final days of waiting by making a sign for my car window saying, "Honk if you love U2" and listed all my planned concert dates on the posterboard. As a final touch, I taped the phrase "U2001" on my back window and polished my license plates which read "U2OPIA."

Finally, March 28th arrived, and I hit the road heading south. It felt incredible to be out on my own, free from work for a few days. The sun shone in through my windshield and I fielded honks in response to my sign with a smile and a peace sign. Once or twice, I looked over and as I was raising my hand I found the driver in the car next to me making the same motion with his own hand. These communications warmed me with the common understanding that a shared interest can engender between strangers. I basked in this warmth as a winding, tree shadowed road stretched before me and lead the way to my friend Cate's home in Charlotte. She had been with me at St. Louis PopMart on my 21st birthday and she was looking forward to seeing another U2 show.

I stopped just south of Richmond and tried to capture the moment in my journal.

I wrote:

It's a beautiful morning for a road trip…I'm sleepy but very happy. Driving along, singing to Achtung Baby, underneath the clear blue sky in the U2-mobile. I'm daydreaming as I ride along this two-lane highway. Dreaming of the concert, the live music, the Bono. The fans, the crowd, the cheering, and the smiles that will fill that arena tomorrow night. I'm basking in the thought of this impending magic.

I arrived at Cate's home on schedule, and we spent the evening catching up and playing with her doll of a daughter. When the clock read the hour for sleep, despite my road weary bones, my mind was spinning with the possibilities of the day that waited on the other side of slumber. I had waited three and a half years for another U2 concert. Like a broken record, lyrics of longing from Pop's "The Playboy Mansion" played over and over in my mind.

When the PopMart tour had ended in 1997, I grieved the muse's departure, and mourned the lost community of fans that I had encountered so briefly. Now the residual emptiness would be filled again. I had no doubts. I knew that the music would come through for me. It was no wonder that sleep did not come easy that night.

When the day of show number one arrived, I found myself filled with a kind of anxious let down. After so many months of waiting for this show, all I really wanted to do was kick back with a few pints to calm my frazzled nerves. I drove to the venue and planned to meet up with my friend Cate later, as she and her friends had separate seats from me. I stopped at a nearby bar and put down a couple pints of Guinness. I caught a shuttle to the Charlotte Colosseum and procured the first signatures in my fan signature book from those fellow drinkers surrounding me.

At the venue I found my seat in the stands and surveyed the scene. I was delighted with the stage set up which was accentuated by a lovely red heart-shaped runway that hugged almost the entire front half of the general admission crowd. I studied the fans lucky enough to be moving in and out of the enclosure. I hoped that I too would experience this show from within the heart later, possibly even tomorrow night in Atlanta. As I settled in, I became aware of a mild hint of claustrophobia. The walls of the arena pressed in, closing around the stage and the audience, bottling up the growing energy. It didn't feel right to put U2 in a box: up to that point I'd only seen the band play at outdoor venues.

When the time finally came and the lads climbed the stairs on to the stage, house lights were still up, and I had a few more pints in my belly. My hand floated up to my mouth covering a huge grin, as I caught the first glimpse of Bono in the flesh. I was elevated by the sight of him from the first faraway glimpse. The show went on, and I found myself so thrilled (in a tipsy way) that I had to run off for a pee and call Ro on my mobile: "Honey, they're here! Bono and The Edge are here and so am I! Can you hear them playing? They're here! They're here!" It was a good night, though the band cut the show short for unknown reasons, playing only nineteen songs instead of their usual twenty plus.

With the next morning's dawn, I bundled my hungover self back into my car, and grabbed a fast-food bite before I set out for Atlanta. As I waited to get back on the Interstate, a young man in a baseball cap honked and waved then jumped out of his car and ran up to my window, saying, "hey were you at the show last night? Are you following them? Where are they going next? That's so cool! When will they be in New York?"

These were good vibes alright.

After another long drive, I made it into Atlanta. I met up with my friends Scottie and Clara from college. We headed to their place, and I got my get up on for the unveiling of the Belly Dancer. Within thirty minutes I was fully decked out in my costume. All grins and glitter. After shooting a few requisite photos, Scottie and I headed out the door and jumped on the subway to the Phillips Arena. I got some stares as we clomped on towards the arena and I pulled my sheer golden cloak closer in around my shoulders, peeking mysteriously at the oglers as I billowed by. Once we got to the arena and found the queue for general admission ticket holders, I spotted some of my mailing list buddies at the top of the line. I chit chatted with a fellow dressed up as Bono's alter ego of circa 1992, The Fly. Sadly, they couldn't let us jump the line, so we tromped past seemingly thousands of fans already waiting for the show, which wasn't scheduled to start for another three hours. My mind was racing, "Can we still get into the heart? Will we? Will we?"

After many highly tense moments, we found ourselves galloping down the stairs to the entrances to the inner sanctum which I had scoped out the evening before in Charlotte. We were given special wristbands and happily joined the sparse crowd that was allowed into the inner stage area at that point. I twirled and danced and took photos and ate a giant pretzel as we waited for the show to start. I wasn't the only dressed up freak, mind you. There was the guy who thought he could pass for Bono as The Fly, and another guy who seemed to think, even more so, that he could pass for The Edge. Fake Edge wore the woolen hat, goatee, red number seven shirt, and all. Other fans serenaded me with lines from "Mysterious Ways" as I sashayed about appropriately in my gold and red silken attire.

Then, the show...And what a mind-blowing experience this time. The show from inside the heart tonight felt exactly like I thought seeing U2 in a nightclub might feel, and in a nightclub with special walkways where the performers move about the periphery, with the added benefit of a crowd outside surrounding and pumping up the energy levels. The intimacy of the view from inside the heart was incredible. The band seemed on fire tonight. It was perhaps the presence of REM in the audience that had the guys kicking up a notch, as well as Ali Hewson. I did my best to advertise my presence as honorary belly dancer, short of throwing a scarf on stage. The people in the crowd around me were urging me to do some actual belly dancing, so during "Sweetest Thing" I found a clear circle and spun and twisted and shook my booty as best I could. There was a soft yellow light shining down on the heart's crowd and it felt as if I were onstage too. It felt as if I were part of the show again, as I had been that night back in '97. It was wonderful.

Scottie, having never been to a U2 concert before, was immediately converted to fan status. A drummer himself, he especially admired Larry's prowess. We hung about outside the arena afterwards chatting and marveling in the post-show afterglow. At my request, he entered one of the first of many beautiful reflections in my "What makes YOU elevate" fan book:

Amongst the crowd the multitudes were seen,

So amazing the truth, $18.38 for the pizza

The truth such a lime, green amongst the multitude,

Back to the amazing, the inspiring, past pop—with truth

How can one band bring so many people to one place?

Fucking Amazing—Destiny Manifest

Then home and pass out time on the couch.

The next morning, I awoke and glanced at the clock. Panicking at the late hour, I hit the road for Blacksburg, Virginia, about a seven-hour drive from Atlanta. I stayed overnight there with another dear friend from college and gushed endlessly about my adventures of the past two days and my plans for more.

Following these two wonderful evenings I was nothing if not ready for more. I went back to Fairfax, VA, and floated back into work. I was rather refreshed by the break and the temporary sense of freedom and adventure, but oh my, was I antsy for the big drive to Chicago, to begin in May. I got busy booking hotel rooms and ordering trip routings from my motor club. I even called Ticketmaster to check for ticket availability, and on a whim, bought a behind-the-stage ticket to the show in Milwaukee, WI on May 9th (this would take me about 400 miles out of my way, but what the hell). The day before I left, I was surprised by my nervousness about making the 700-plus-mile drive out to Chicago on my own. Oh, I was excited, but I was nervous too.

Early on the morning of May 6, Ro woke me up and gave me a stuffed kitty to keep me company on the road. I set Kitty on my dashboard and was off, north towards the Pennsylvania Turnpike with coffee in hand. I left early, before sunrise, so that I could make the six-hour drive and arrive in Pittsburgh in plenty of time to check into my hostel, find the Mellon Arena, and start queuing. What I didn't count on was a freaking marathon which had the Pittsburgh thoroughfares all cordoned off and screwed up, so that I was directed by a policeman to go the opposite direction than that which my directions to the hostel indicated. Damn! Pittsburgh seemed a crap city to drive in on a normal day, let alone when there's a freaking marathon going on. I encountered all kinds of one-way streets and bridges and one-way bridges and tunnels that lead to God knows where, but possibly hell. Out of desperation, I rang the hostel for better directions, but of course the desk boy was just as confused as me due to the screwy blockage of the streets. Multiple phone calls, many a wrong turn, 20 minutes, and $30 worth of roaming charges later, I finally found my digs for the night. I hauled my frazzled butt inside and moved on to the next challenge: how to get to the venue.

I decided to walk.

It was a lovely stroll down the huge hillside in Pittsburgh that overlooks the city, with a tram going up and down for tourists. I had been to Pittsburgh once before; the city's certain industrial charm and grit felt comfortingly familiar. I gazed down upon the river running through the city and huge arching bridges spanning the waters and leading towards the downtown area, the houses set up on the hillside with staircases instead of sidewalks moving between them. It was rather odd, looking just down to my right into someone's backyard, seemingly hundreds of feet below, and seeing their wash blowing in the spring breeze. Luckily, I found the Arena with no problem (way to go, feet!) and circled it looking for the line in. I met a couple of fans on the way in standing near the garage entrance. I asked them where the GA line was, and they pointed me in the right direction. The level of excitement in me increased as we chatted. One of them had been at the show in Lexington two nights ago, and still seemed to be riding the residual high. I thanked them and scurried off in search of my place in line.

It was 12 noon, and I was rather surprised to see upwards of 100 early comers already queued up and hunkered down to wait out the afternoon until doors opened around 6:00 p.m. It was an unseasonably warm and pleasant day, but I was knackered from having gotten up so early and still residually stressed from the headache of finding the hostel, not to mention absurdly excited. Adrenaline coursed through me as I took in this welcome scene. I sat myself down at the end of the line of fans and leaned awkwardly against a concrete wall.

Thus began one hell of a miserable afternoon. It must have been just from sleep deprivation and overexcitement, but it was pretty much a horrible and tedious time right from the start. I looked longingly at the people in the front of the line (rumor had it that they had started queuing 8:00 a.m...this seemed insane to me), who were set up with hammocks in the shade. I didn't even have a damn newspaper. I managed to amuse myself somewhat by watching the tour trucks in the underground garage area, which was on the other side of and below the concrete ledge doubling as my backrest (what luxury!). After a couple hours I realized the other vital component that I had forgotten. *Sunblock*. Well, who would have thought? It was barely past April! Regardless, the sun was beating down on us and temperatures were pleasantly hot. I was enjoying the warmth in a tank top only, as I was soon too warm to wear the light hoodie I had as cover. Soon enough, my flesh was none too pleasantly fried. To top it off, I discovered that I had been sitting in a nice puddle of melting tar, which was adhering to the butt-crack of my shorts as well as the light khaki of my hoodie. Yikes.

By the time 6:00 p.m. rolled around, I had struck up a lukewarm rapport with the college-aged couple sitting next to me. I think they were as annoyed as I was, but at least they had each other. All I had was my tarred shorts. By now, the line of GA ticket holders had stretched all the way down to the end of the concrete wall, spilling out on to the sidewalk, and down adjacent to that parking area I had been studying earlier. The people at the end of the line looked at least a mile away from us up front. This provided minimal comfort to me after having gotten through the lousy afternoon. I was so fried, exhausted, and generally uncomfortable, that as it grew closer to show time and we were going nowhere, I joked to my new friends about ending it all by jumping the concrete wall to my death: "I can't take it anymore!" I could picture the media byte vividly: *Crazed music fan suffers heat induced hysteria and ends life: band dedicates song and reminds concert goers of the importance of sunblock. Story at 11.* When the line finally did move inside, a cheer went up and a bit of energy came to me from god knows where.

Once inside, I grabbed a spot alone the railing inside the heart. So tired. Don't know if I'll make it. Must drink beer. I got a beer and suffered through PJ Harvey's set. I was not impressed with Polly Jean that day. I was excited but flagging. After the show, the only things I could really recall from the concert were; A: Bono slapping hands with someone a few spots down from me on the railing and then commencing a game of rock-paper-scissors with him, reaching across the no man's land between stage and floor, and B: cramping up so badly during the first encore that I had to leave the show and hit a dirty ladies room stall, where I sat moaning, head plopped in my hands. Once I made it out of the stall, I was confronted with lobster-red face, shoulders, and chest in the mirror. I looked like a dying refugee. I did not go back into the show after that. Instead, I went outside and joined a small cluster of fans waiting for the band's exit at the ramp to the underground entrance.

I spotted Paul McGuinness, and next thing you know, there went U2, zipping past in their limos. Only Edge was gracious enough to honor us with a halfhearted wave, and then the comfy bastards had zipped off to their private jet or some other exquisitely heavenly non-sunburnt place.

I commenced looking for a cab. Of course, I couldn't find one for nearly an hour, and by then I was a blithering idiot, scared and alone wandering the streets of Pittsburgh at night, a rape victim waiting to happen. And you know what else really was bitterly ironic? By then I was *too cold*. Finally, I made it home to the hostel and I crashed. Hard.

I woke up the next morning in a strange little hostel room, still feeling dead tired and in lots of pain from the sunburn. I stumbled out of the hostel at about 11:00 a.m. and found my vehicle. Thumbing through the local paper, looking for last night's review, I heard a tap on my window. There was a young Latin fellow with a rucksack. He was standing next to my car with an inquisitive look on his face. He said, "Are you Marcella?" I admitted to the charge. He told me he got my first name from the hostel folk and that he was a fellow U2 geek in search of a ride to the next show in Columbus, Ohio. After a short moment's check in with common sense, I chose to ditch my better judgment in the name of good U2-ey vibes and offered the young man a ride with me to the next stop.

Cesar and I came into each other's company with a comfort that is uncommon when one is confronted with an unfamiliar person. Here is where I had my first real taste of the camaraderie and sense of unity that grows out of the concert experience. It's not completely unique to U2, but there's something unique about the feeling that can exist out of nowhere between U2 fans. Rock shows, at their best, are an expression of ideas and emotion. Some of us are drawn to music because it pulls our insides out and sets us free of our isolation. This kind of soul music is abundant, and it comes in many forms. When the soul is present in music, it speaks clearly to those that can hear it: those who understand and identify with the essential things expressed by the soul given voice through art. The voice of the soul in music takes on a presence in concert (if the artist is up to it that night), and kindred spirits are freed to dance together to the rhythm that they find in a tacit understanding. This is a connection that is like the passion of lovemaking or the ecstasy of transcendence. It's beyond words.

If you can dig all that, then maybe you can understand how Cesar and I were able to feel comfortable together. It was very nice to have good company that day, for weariness was still upon me and the constant flow of adrenaline through my veins had me feeling rather burnt out.

Once we hit Columbus, I grabbed a hotel room and we headed to the venue. Crisis number one of the evening: Clever Marcy has forgotten her ticket. After consulting with a few scalpers, I looked upon the growing GA line in a torrent of anxiety, asked Cesar to try and hold my spot, and took off for the hotel again. Cesar had problems as well; being that he did not have a ticket at all, being that he had decided on a lark to hitch a ride with me to Ohio, being that he was from Peru and visiting relatives in New York (it all made sense at the time).

With crisis number one averted, I returned to site and sat in line with Cesar for the next two hours. I passed my fan book around and got a few signatures to add to the collection. Soon enough we were herded in through the GA entrance and Cesar and I did the speed-walk-jog-"don't run"-trot one does when one is trying to get to the front of the stage and security is yelling at one not to run. We were counted off in the last few people who made it into the heart, and we awaited our admission. As we stood at the tail end of the herd okayed to enter the inner sanctum, my gaze wandered about the National Arena. My eyes came to rest upon who else but Mr. Paul McGuinness, strolling about the side stage area, just separated from us by a waist high railing.

I grabbed Cesar and whispered, "That's Paul McGuinness!" Then, without thinking, I blurted out "Hi Paul!" Amicably, he wandered over to where we were waiting and asked Cesar and I, "Is security treating you all fairly?" We said yes, and I mentioned that I only waited two hours today compared to six yesterday in Pittsburgh. We exchanged a bit of small talk including a "you're going to how many shows??" sort of comment from Mr. McGuinness. I showed him my "What makes YOU elevate?" fan signature book. He checked it out, and signed it, writing about "Columbus the home of the Qube." Then Cesar and I were off into the heart.

Cesar and I camped out as close to the rail as we could, on Adam's side. We goofed around with our neighbors as we enjoyed the pre-show tingle.

Unfortunately, after about an hour of enjoying said tingle, Cesar pointed out to me that I was missing the inside-the-heart-elite wristband. I decided to seek out a security guard to ask for my rightful wristband. To make a long story short, this was a bad move: Mr. Flat Top Security Guard kicked me out of the heart and left me in tears. I was yelling, "This is not fucking fair!" as he forcibly escorted me from the heart because some dumb ass failed to give me my wristband when I entered. Essentially, I was paying for their fuck-up and wow I was so mad that I couldn't stop crying hysterically throughout the next thirty to forty minutes, which was how long it took to get me back in. It seemed that insisting repeatedly to any security staff that would listen that one had a conversation with the band's manager pre-show about how fairly security was treating the fans and repeating the word "supervisor" will eventually get one somewhere. More likely, they just wanted me to shut up, and didn't give a damn about my rantings.

 Eventually, I was escorted back into the heart with Cesar. We enjoyed an excellent show with our new compadres at Adam's rail. I enjoyed watching Adam smile down at us, making eye contact and laughing at some silliness a fan offered him. The rest of the band tended to be such an intense bunch onstage, that sharing the show with Adam so close lent a refreshingly different vibe. We were swept up in the fun down front and having a blast by the time "Streets" and "Pride" closed out the first set. Following the concert, Cesar and I milled about outside the National Arena with thousands of departing concertgoers, searching with no luck for the exit from which the band might still emerge for meet and greet. We staked out some snacks and water and shared our own stories of the inspiration that comes from the show, and the music, and the people. All the negative energy from the stressful past two days had dissolved completely by then; even the mini trauma of being kicked out of the heart.

 Cesar had nowhere to go afterwards except maybe the airport, so I allowed him to accompany me home to the hotel room where I lent him a blanket and the floor. The next morning, when we woke up it was off to the airport for him and on to Milwaukee for me. That day I drove no less than ten hours out of my way so as not to miss the next night's show.

After a much-needed respite on the off night of May 8th, I woke up feeling better than I had in years, or perhaps ever. I got in the car and drove through the clear sunny spring morning northwest into Wisconsin. The contented feeling that washed over me was a combination of a good night's sleep and the inexplicable good vibes that take one over only when a spiritual need is fulfilled. The tension and trauma of the last few days had slipped away and was replaced with a peaceful sense of vast awareness. I felt a Buddha like calm and contentedness. I smiled to myself as I drove by Cheeseville, a small town near the big city, and other such thematic and stately establishments. Milwaukee charmed me as I rolled into the city and followed easy directions to the Hotel Wisconsin. I checked into a very old, never been renovated high-rise hotel in the downtown district and waited for some guys to fix the elevator. Once they did, I dropped my bags in a small musty room on one of the upper floors and headed off to find the venue.

On the way there, I ran into Charlie, a fan I had met in Pittsburgh. He was staying in a hotel near mine and was heading back down to the GA scene after a brief respite. I shared the walk down to the arena with Charlie and took in my first sights of Milwaukee. We traded stories of our adventures and talked about plans for the Indianapolis show tomorrow, where he promised to try to save me a spot near him in the GA line.

Milwaukee was one of the only towns in which I was holding reserved seats as opposed to general admission, and I intended to use the opportunity of an afternoon free of holding a spot in a long line to try and squeeze in a quick encounter with the band. Soon Charlie and I parted ways at the venue, wishing each other a good show as he headed back to the line. I scoped out the arena and found what seemed to be the most likely band entrance point, where a small cluster of fans gathered. They wore the same nervous look that I felt on my face, and they clutched at various and sundry U2 paraphernalia: album sleeves, CDs, flowers to give the band, etc. One woman held a wrapped gift bearing Bono's name on the tag, because tomorrow, May 10th, was the man's 41st birthday. I chatted the afternoon away with the other fans waiting patiently by the entrance, under the watchful gaze of the security guards. After the previous show's incident, I was feeling none too friendly with the yellow-shirted-wannabe-power-tripping freaks. I bumped into a bloke named Mike with whom I had exchanged a few pre-tour emails and ideas: for example, Bono's birthday night concert plans and scenarios.

Mike and I talked shop for a while as the day grew overcast, and I gave into folly by bumming a smoke off another fan, taking the first step in a series that would ultimately lead to my defeat in a battle with nicotine addiction which I had been waging for the past six months. So, Mike and I smoked and chatted, chatted and smoked, and stood and stood in a companionable silence off and on for the next two hours. Here was a fan more dedicated (or perhaps just wealthier? Or maybe a little more psycho? Perhaps all of the above), than yours truly. This man was an Australian who lived in England. He would fly back and forth across the Atlantic three times this year to get to a total of 27 shows. It's hard in situations like that to avoid asking those questions that just hang in the air begging for an answer: how in God's name are you paying for all this? What the hell kind of job do you have anyway? Somehow tact got the better of me and an uncomfortable situation was avoided.

Eventually, as rain rolled in, I gave up, told Mike I hoped to see him again soon (it was inevitable, really), and went off to forage for food. I found myself back near the Hotel Wisconsin at a dingy but endearing diner where I ordered a meal and wrote in my tour log in the only writing utensil I had on me, a red marker.

Walking back to the arena, I enjoyed a very real sense for the first time that I was on the road with the circus, following the song of the siren that others celebrated as the tunes blew through town. I strolled past bars and pubs filled with pre-concert drinkers and photographed the revelers and the pub chalkboards advertising $1 off drinks for concert goers in front of establishments blasting U2 of old and new from their speakers. This city I had never visited suddenly felt like home.

After entering the venue, I found my seat in the $45 reserved seating section, the only seat I had been able to score at the last-minute addition of this stop with the traveling show. These lower price seats were located behind the stage on the second tier of the arena. There was no view of the four screens focused on the band members nor was there one of the ten-foot-high screens that rose from the back of the stage. I spent the show shooting photos that didn't develop and depleting an already low level of energy as I jumped, dance, and wriggled about by no free will of my own. The music grabbed me and yanked me around even as my ability to tolerate this level of stimulation seemed to be weakening. I spotted Charlie easily; he was in the second row of people at the tip of the heart (way down there…but he was rather tall and stood out of the mish mosh of reaching hands and shining faces). It was nice seeing a familiar face in the outer frame of Bono's spotlight throughout the show.

I left the show a little early during "One," being less than thrilled with my crappy ass seat…And I went off to find the exit to the arena, hoping to catch yet another glimpse of the magical music makers on their way out of the arena tonight.

I was a little troubled about those crappy seats. What kind of plan was that anyway? To have been able to see squat at these shows, one had to be able to either: A) pay a minimum of $85 per seat or, B) spend at least several hours waiting around in total discomfort for these boys to grace us with their presence. What was up with that? I didn't understand why U2 would put their fans in this position. I liked the GA set up, I really did, but only because I had worked it out for me, personally, to reliably get into the heart. However, it was a hell of an investment in time, energy, and money. Not every rock fan has those resources.

At the same time, I realize there isn't anything fair about rock music. It is what it is, and you can accept it, or you can fuck off. That's the beauty of it.

I left the Milwaukee show in search of the getaway vehicles. The show had passed with little out of the ordinary (especially from the viewpoint of the crappy ass seats). We were graced with Bono's premature rendition of "Happy Birthday" to himself towards the end of the show. As I ran out towards the exit, I spotted a half dozen fans standing by what appeared to be the exit gate (including a girl with a cowboy hat and a sign that said, "I have a weakness for Irishmen," alluding to Bono's one time remark that he had a certain weakness for belly dancers). Next thing I knew we were all hauling ass around the corner, as we spotted about four black town cars being ushered out quickly by a police escort. We all ran after them lustily, cowboy hat girl holding her hat on her head, and we visibly sagged as they shot off into the darkness.

On the walk back to the hotel, I ran into Charlie. He was grinning mightily and glowing visibly as he proudly displayed a harmonica. He happily reported that Bono had passed it down to him from the stage. The man seemed thrilled, and I was happy for him, and jealous. We exchanged ideas and plans for tomorrow night's birthday show in Indianapolis, to which I had my very own GA ticket, and a lovely bag of birthday tricks up my sleeve…or in the trunk of my car. With tired but happy shouts of "See ya in Indy!" we waved goodbye. I smiled myself to sleep that night in my creepy old hotel room.

I woke up the next morning to a jarring ring from the hotel phone. That's right, I remembered groggily, I had requested a wake-up call. I was too tired to get my butt out of bed. I rolled out about two hours later and put my sleepy self behind the wheel. And I'm not kidding about sleepy…I had a frighteningly hard time keeping myself awake on the nine-hour drive from Milwaukee to Indianapolis. We mustn't forget that I was heading towards the fourth strange city on my solo tour. I wasn't doing a stellar job of taking care of myself. Remember that evil sunburn from Pittsburgh? By the morning of May 10th, I was a frightening semblance of red peeling flesh. I was hurting, but still, what I think of when I remember that day is a feeling of sublime contentment.

I feel now that I must have been experiencing some sort of low-level buzz of enlightenment, as alluded to earlier. You know those moments where you're doing, being, feeling the moment and nothing else? All my cares had become insignificant as I realized that I was exactly where and what I wanted to be. Yes, I was struggling physically, but somehow, I was mentally, and spiritually, wide awake to everything. The colors of the morning were crisp and bright as the sun shone on the dashboard and the highway stretched on before me.

Even as I pulled in at a highway rest stop and took a nap (the alternative would have been a much longer "nap" in a quiet Indiana field), I felt more alive than I could remember feeling in a very long time.

Driving into Indy, I was pleasantly relieved to find that the Conseco Fieldhouse (the location of tonight's show) was well marked off the highway. I was beginning to trust myself a little more after having survived the Pittsburgh mix-up, having since been through three much simpler towns. Still, I carried that East Coast defensiveness about driving in unknown territories. But it was a quiet and secure defensiveness, based on a knowledge that nothing awful could possibly happen to me in my own safe homeland. I drove into the glistening, flat metropolis of Indianapolis and found my way to the showgrounds for the night.

Since it was around 3:00 p.m. when I got to the GA line, said line had already grown to a healthy size. I toted my bag of birthday goodies with me, which held over one hundred paper birthday hats purchased at a party supply store in Fairfax VA, and a lovely sign I had toiled on in preparation for this evening. The sign had held up nicely through the drive and still glittered its message: "Happy 41st birthday Bono! Dance with this Party Girl!" I had been compelled to make a poster to wave for at least one of these shows. I had a very good feeling about what a sparkly poster can do to catch an idol's eye.

I trundled down the line and observed the familiar sight of fans in varying stages of repose, mounting fatigue, and encampment. Most of the folks in front had set themselves up for a moderate level of comfort for their hours of lying-in-wait for show time. I scanned the line for Charlie but did not see him, so with no other option, I plodded past the dozens of fans who had gotten there before me and claimed my spot at the end. I felt pretty sure that my spot in the heart was secured, but still slightly nervous.

At first the line was mellow, but as the hours wore on from my arrival at 3:00 p.m., I soon got to know those waiting in line nearest me. Being solitary, I found myself sitting on the ground next to a woman about my age and on her own, who sat reading quietly. Throughout the next hour typical moments of communication amongst perfect strangers finding themselves stuck in line occurred, and about two hours before the doors to the arena opened, I found myself amongst friends. In addition to the solitary reading girl, there were two Texan couples just behind us in line who shared our excitement. The women were tiny blondes with thick drawls. We traded stories and made predictions about whether we would get into the heart.

As the mood in the line got more festive, our numbers grew quickly, and I began passing out birthday hats to those who would take them. Most of the people in front of me knew well that it was Bono's birthday. Many were constructing various posters appropriate to the occasion. One person ahead of me had the same hat idea; about a dozen of the show goers before us already had their birthday hats in hand. I merrily passed out hats to those who didn't yet have them as the line continued to swell with excitement. I walked the length of the queue and passed my new friends with what was left in my stash, continuing to distribute green and pink hats. The number of waiters had doubled since I had arrived two hours ago, and more and more folks were making their way to jump on the end.

I did find Charlie in this later surveying of the line, and despite our earlier conversation we both knew that I had arrived too late to jump in line with him. I was also disappointed to realize I had forgotten my happy birthday balloons. These small slip ups did minimal damage to my mood as we waited for the doors to open on Bono's birthday party.

Much small talk and giddy chatter with the ladies on the line and the girl who had been reading beside me, and several cigarettes later, we found ourselves finally starting to move. What a beautiful moment that is…remember when you were eight years old, and you've been waiting in the line at Disneyworld for Space Mountain for what seems like days, but was probably no more than one hour, and finally, the gate opens and you're about to step into the seat of the rollercoaster? It was just like that.

A funny thing happened with this line though. The security folks really screwed it up, and it worked to my advantage immensely. There had been about 240 people ahead of me. They herded us into a lobby sort of area in the Conseco Fieldhouse, en masse, and we were given wristbands about eight at a time. At that point, the line started milling about and it turned into a blob. The blob was then herded to the left side of the lobby… about 100 people probably went that way until some folks started going to the right down a different hall. Being a fly-by-the-seat-of-my-pants sort of girl, my new reader friend (hereafter referred to as Mary) and I trotted around the corner with the little blonde Texan ladies and waited around there at a gate. We were maybe twenty people back in the mob around this gate. Within a few moments, the gate was opened, we were directed down the hall, through an entryway, and the arena opened around us. I descended with my friends down the stairs through the Golden Circle seats and was thrilled to see that *there was next to no one* down on the floor yet.

There is no sight quite like the empty arena two hours before showtime, at that moment when the first fans are let in, and they converge on the stage and the heart-shaped catwalk like grains of sand squeezing through the hourglass. There hangs in the air the smell of anticipation, and potential, and…joy waiting to happen.

We trotted down to the arena floor, and while all the twenty people who had been ahead of us ran to the heart, I grabbed Mary, and we made a beeline to the tip of the heart. I could not believe it: I managed to stake a claim at a spot on the rail where I was resting my elbows on a little ledge. The very ledge that Bono stood on during "Until the End of the World," where he would reach out and taunt the crowd, who would, in turn, reach up and grab him, supporting his weight, and basically getting the chance to look up his nose. Despite, or more honestly, perhaps due to, the imminent danger of getting a close-up of Bono's nasal passages, I was thrilled.

A moment after we staked our claim, my good friend Charlie appeared and chose a fine spot for concert viewing pleasure right behind us. Luckily, Charlie was quite tall, so I did not worry about standing in front of a man who I knew had been far ahead of me in line. As for everyone else, bummer for them. There was no way we could have straightened things out at that point (for that I was grateful). We sat around and bought beers from the vendors who milled about as we watched the arena fill up. The fans continued to pour in and find their spots in the tiers of reserved seating and on the concrete floor stretching behind us. I saved Mary's spot as she ran off to get her heart wristband, "just in case," and Charlie and Mary saved mine as I ran off to empty my bladder. Upon my return, I proceeded to consume two more beers and enjoyed the spectacle of the arena filling up.

As the floor got more flooded, we stood up and held on tight to our few feet of prime railing. We swayed subtly with the movement of the masses surrounding us. We gazed straight across the catwalk at the fans on the front lines there, and into the heart where we waved at our Texan friends who were hopping about and grinning wildly. I saw Mike standing quietly amongst a clump of folks chilling in the more spacious part of the heart towards the back but away from the rails. For him it was just another night. I was fascinated with everyone around me. There was a guy with glasses standing directly to my left and I smiled at him, and we chatted. He was from Luxembourg and his name was Christian. I asked him how many shows he had been to, and he said to me, "All of them." I was pleased to have found yet another kindred spirit. I asked, how many was he planning to go to, and Christian said, "All of them…except maybe Detroit." This amused me. He couldn't explain why Detroit had been singled out as one to miss.

Then the lights went out and PJ did her stuff. I was still lukewarm about Miss Harvey's music, but Christian seemed to enjoy her quite a lot. Then passed the additional forty-five minutes of celebratory waiting as the lights came back up and the tunes playing through the sound system. The balloons bobbled about the arena as concert goers drank and danced, and the beer bottles piled up on the ledge where Bono would likely stand during the rapidly approaching show. The fans lining the outer edge of the heart wore birthday hats, and many of the posters I had seen being constructed earlier were now being waved about playfully. I was happy to see that my vision of a birthday hat wearing crowd had come to fruition both by my own planning efforts and parallel efforts at people I didn't even know.

Then began the chords of the concert version of "Elevation:" that low gong and glistening sound of the introductory notes of the song… the cheers erupting as Adam…Larry…Edge…and finally Bono, took their places on stage. The lights blazed and we all regarded each other happily; fans and fans, fans and band, band and band. The energy swirled and grew on itself as it bounced around the room. The crowd soaked up the rebounding energy and bounced right along with it.

As usual, early in the show, Bono made his way out to visit the crowd around the tip of the heart. I found myself standing a few feet from the end of the catwalk, and I was eye level with Bono's feet as they sauntered down in our direction. A fan along the catwalk on the side of the heart threw glitter at the man as he smirkingly regarded us all lined up in our party hats with our happy birthday signs on either side of him. Shouting out happily to the arena that tonight was his birthday party, he grabbed the bag of glitter from the fan and poured it over himself, saying, "Now I thought you didn't like all the glitter and the glam." Later, during "New York," Bono came back out all the way to the tip and stood a few feet in front of us. I held my sign up into his spotlight and he looked it over, giving me a little smirk and a nod. Charlie clapped me on the shoulder from behind and said, "He just read your sign!" *I know*, I thought to myself as my heart raced in my chest, envisioning a forthcoming dance in the spotlight with Bono to the strains of "Party Girl."

For the next full hour of songs, we partied at the tip of the heart and lost ourselves in the show. At one point the star stepped out onto the ledge that had been our temporary beer bottle rack and leaned over us into the crowd. I grabbed an ankle and held on (until he tried to move and then I let go…Obviously, right?). Later, Bono knelt before us during the intro to "Streets," and read out a Psalm as he did every night:

What can I give back to God,

For the blessings He has poured out on me?...

I lift high a cup of salvation in a toast to Our Father

And follow through on a promise I made to Him

These words were quietly breathed to the thousands of fans hushed with the awesome opening of the song, as gentle jangling chords filled the arena and a red glow emanated from the stage. Edge began picking out the solitary shimmering notes. Then, as the music picked up, like dawn breaking on the horizon, Bono stood above us as the house lights blazed on, and again all the thousands of us regarded each other in the brightly lit celebration. As the music built and the bass took over, Bono seemed to feed off the energy and again took his sprint around the heart-shaped catwalk. When he left, I watched the security guard quietly hand a female fan down front with us the sheet of paper from which Bono had read the Psalm.

During "Mysterious Ways," another notable event occurred. It seemed quite run of the mill at first, when the show man (shaman?) chose a woman from the crowd and danced merrily all the way around the heart with her. They came around the back of the stage and out again to the tip, arms slung about each other's shoulders companionably. Then, before thought, Bono was reaching out to a girl on the rail, inviting her, too, up to dance. Then, in an instant, a third…and Bono was shouting out over the continuing rumble of song, "Hey! It's my birthday! Any girls out there wanna dance, come on up!" Now, a fourth, as they continued to approach, and the fourth had been standing just to my right. At this point I was in Pogo stick mode. As the growing crowd of partiers led by Bono passed me by, I jumped heartily and attempted to boost myself over the rail, repeatedly, to no avail. Until out of nowhere: my butt was being supported by an anonymously helpful fan, and my foot was up on the railing. I went scrambling across the security pit between fans and stage. Then I was up, dancing across the surprisingly wide catwalk belly dancer style (or so I tried), wearing my birthday hat and hatching a plan to give it to the birthday boy with a birthday hug. I followed the women, who had grown to over a dozen, and were still climbing up onto the catwalk. We grooved around the heart, en masse. I looked down on Edge, Adam, and Larry, as we passed along the raised catwalk just behind the stage. Edge and Adam appeared to be laughing, as Larry seemed to remain focused solely on his drumming with his trademark stern determination. We cornered round stage right and I gazed up for a moment at the hundreds of fans cheering down at us from the upper right reserved seating section. I notice that the catwalk was marked with strategically placed X's. And then, that was all. Bono was kissing and hugging the ladies goodbye and scooting back towards the main stage as we all piled off, glowing with pleasure.

Mary was beaming when I returned, "I'm so glad you got up there!" she said. Charlie, too, congratulated me. I just grinned throughout the remainder of the finale. As Mary and I followed the rest of the crowd out of the arena after showtime, we ranted and raved about how much fun it had been. We exchanged email addresses and she spoke of catching another show next month. I promised to write her before we hugged goodbye and parted ways into the Indianapolis night. Just hours before, Mary and I had been perfectly solitary, and even aloof, strangers. After this show we felt like old friends reunited and parting again after too short a time. I hope to see her again down the road.

After getting lost one more time in post-concert traffic, I retained my glow as I journaled in my quiet hotel room:

I just can't stop smiling…Can't get over the memory of that lap, dancing around the heart with Bono in the lead of all the ladies. What a week this has been…what a week! The glitter, the party hats, the signs, the choruses of Happy Birthday…what a show!

Waking up the next morning, my body ached with fatigue. My glow, however, remained, and I happily checked out of the Holiday Inn of Indianapolis, grabbing a newspaper, and reading last night's review over a solo brunch.

With the party that was last night's show fresh in my mind, I hopped in the U2-mobile and hit the road for Chicago, where I was scheduled to pick up my brother Chris and his new wife Bobsie at O'Hare airport. I would take them to a U2 concert with tickets I had purchased as their long since promised wedding present.

Navigating through the late afternoon Chicago traffic that Friday was less than thrilling, but I had been doing so well since Pittsburgh with the driving that I managed to refrain from panicking. I made it to O'Hare safely and sat on an airport bench by luggage claim where I wrote in my journal and savored my final moments of solitude. The last time I had been at O'Hare, Chris had been the one picking me up at the drop from a bus ride from Madison WI, where I had been at a U2 show two nights ago. This time it was me picking up big brother to see the show in Chicago.

I settled into a comfortable sense of self as I observed things coming full circle. I found it strange that though so many things had changed over the years, this strange ritual had repeated itself almost a tee. I hoped that Chris and I would always meet in Chicago to go see a U2 show.

Although hugely pleased to see my brother and his wife, I regretted the end of my solitary journey as real life began to settle back in with their entrance into my adventure. I felt safe again. With that feeling of security within the family's presence, the bright edges of reality faded back into themselves as spontaneity and risk dissolved like mist.

The next morning, aggravation re-entered the picture when Ro called to inform me that he had missed his flight and would be catching a later one. I fretted the morning away and caught an extra nap, sleeping through dreams threaded with anxiety. Several hours later, Bobsie, Chris, and I found Ro's flight arriving at Chicago's Midway Airport. We hid behind airport ads and watched Ro wander around looking for us with his baggage, until Bobsie and I popped out and attacked him with the bear hugs reserved for airport reunions.

The next two hours were fraught with physical complications on my part. At one point, Ro had to run out from our hotel room and pick up some medicine of a rather delicate nature at a local pharmacy. I stayed at the hotel and moaned while he was gone. I had wanted to get to the United Arena early enough to scan the GA line for familiar faces, but, given the combination of Ro's late flight and my inability to move, we didn't get to the venue until the middle of PJ's set.

The evening was mildly tinged with pain for me, both physical and emotional. Physical pain because I was sick, and tired. Emotional pain because I knew I had to leave this magic carpet ride and get back to reality for a few weeks, that I might continue to gainfully support myself as a valuable member of society. Bleh. Who wants to do that when the alternative is complete immersion into rock and roll fantasy? But I had no choice. And to be fair, I really was hurting physically in a great variety of ways. I needed rest. There was no way I could have hung in there for the next three shows in Chicago.

We found our way to our nosebleed seats, where we stood eye level with Bulls pennants hanging from the ceiling of the incredibly massive United Center. It was a drastic change from the view up Bono's nostrils I had had in Indianapolis two nights ago. I enjoyed the new vantage point. The construction of this arena was truly incredible. I marveled at humanity's drive to really get together; to build a shell like this at incredible cost so that we could all be together, sitting like so many bats in a giant cavern.

I gazed down at the bats that were nearest the light source, or the food source, or whatever it is that bats flock to. I saw Mike way down in the heart and pointed my ant-sized friend out to Ro. Then came the show.

It was quite an enthusiastic return to Chicago, punctuated by one more verse of "happy birthday to me" from our egocentric bat hero, Bono. The show was enhanced by two fans from inside the heart who were pulled onstage. The first was a pianist who stood down near the heart's tip holding a poster advertising his talent. He was invited to join Bono and Edge onstage during "Stay." He did a damn good job accompanying the professionals, despite (or perhaps because of?) A blunt warning from Bono: "Do not fuck up."

I could see that there was a girl in the heart dressed up as a belly dancer just as I had been in Atlanta. I was mildly bemused when Bono invited her up onstage to belly dance him around the heart's catwalk during the end of "Mysterious Ways." She did a good job too, and how could I begrudge her the good fortune (even though it had been my idea in Atlanta, and no one had noticed the belly dancer there), when two nights before I had partaken in a birthday conga line?

I initiated what would become a personal tradition that night, as I wept through the closing lines of "Walk On."

My tears of grief for a great week's passing gave way to tears of celebration as the band broke through the "Hallelujah" chorus that ended the live version of "Walk On." The chorus ended the second leg of my U2 tour 2001. With a weepy smile, I waved goodbye to the fans and the music and the band and promised I would be back soon.

CHAPTER THREE:
REVELATION

The next three weeks passed with a flurry of activity in preparation for the third leg of my trip. More hotel rooms were booked, more tickets arrived in the mail, and email communications with other fans online flowed daily. Though I was unable to be there physically, I followed the tour through to the West Coast online. In this way, a whole new world had opened to U2 fans via the Internet. There were newsgroups that discussed each night's show and websites devoted to trading tickets. On the newsgroups we met each other and made plans to meet at the shows. It was through one of these newsgroups that I got wind of a couple who lived outside Albany, New York, who had sent out word on the wire inviting any traveling show goers to stay in their home and enjoy a barbecue on the day of the show.

These people, the Millers, were not asking for anything in return. At all. They posted a link on the newsgroup to an E-vite which allowed folks to RSVP, reserving a bed in their large house, or a piece of floor space, or even a small piece of ground in their backyard upon which to pitch a tent. This newsgroup went out to upwards of 3000 people all over the world. Nameless, faceless people who could only be drawn to receive it by a serious interest in U2. Was it crazy for the Millers to open themselves up in this way? I thought this just might be the case. Yep, I thought they were most likely nuts as I checked off a box to save myself and Ro an actual bedroom in their home. I figured, what the heck, I've got nothing to lose. If Ro hadn't been with me, I probably would have been safe and traditional and booked a room somewhere. But Ro is a big dude, and I figured we would be safe. I was curious to see this thing happen.

It was on the Internet that I searched for someone to trade GA tickets with me for the first Boston show. On one of those trading post sites I posted a message:

HAVE TWO GA FOR 2ND NITE IN BOSTON. WILL TRADE FOR TWO GA FOR 1ST NITE IN BOSTON.

Within the week, I had received a reply from a guy by the name of Marcus saying he would take me up on that. We traded a few tour stories and talked about our plans for Boston, all through an ongoing email swap. After a few friendly exchanges, I wrote saying that I wasn't sure how these Internet trades usually worked...Did we need to use certified mail or some sort of receipt system? Marcus lived in California. How would we physically swap tickets from across the nation without one person risking the loss of these tickets, now going for upwards of $300 at scalper sites?

Marcus put this problem to rest very easily. He told me, not to worry, that he would simply put his tickets in the mail and when I received them, I could mail him the two I had in my possession. *What?* I was floored. I experienced a few moments of initial shock as questions raced through my mind: But how do you know? But I could easily just...Are you sure about this? Are you nuts? I wrote back and thanked him for proving to me that I wasn't the only one who believes that most people are good and trustworthy. I'm not saying that I would do the same thing (I mean, you never know who you're dealing with out there), but I was impressed with his level of trust.

Sure enough, about a week later, I received two GA tickets for the first Boston show. They were sealed in a padded manila envelope that had traveled through your basic USPS, and with them was packed a small surprise. After I pulled out my new pair of tickets, I found in the padded envelope a plain CD sleeve with two discs labeled, "U2: Seattle April 5th, 2001." He had sent me a recording of a show that had taken place earlier in the spring. I was warmed to the core by the kindness of a stranger. I wrote Marcus back to let him know I had received his package and conveyed my gratitude for the concert CDs. We made plans to meet up before the show in Boston for a quick hello, and I dropped his tickets in the mail to him.

This experience nourished the growth of a feeling in me that had been born on the first leg. The feeling was one of wonder and joy at discovering this community of good people who had come out of the woodwork and come to trust one another simply because of a shared interest. Where there was nothing before, I found myself surrounded by a network of friends who seemed to share my level of sensitivity and quiet trust in the good of others.

Across the world, across the nation, these people were given a chance to be together in celebration. We made the most of it. One of the great things about U2's live performance is that the band makes the audience feel an integral part of the show, on many levels. It was the shows that we were all looking forward to, and it was each other that we were also looking forward to. Many of these fans were older and had celebrated together on previous tours. They were coming together again for the first time since PopMart four years ago. They welcomed me warmly into their fold. They offered me understanding, as well as food and lodging, and above all, a form of anonymous and benign love.

I miss them now, you know. We've all retreated to the shadows of our normal lives. We will fall together again when the muse returns.

Before I knew it, the first week of June was upon us. I sheepishly took my seven vacation days and waved goodbye to my colleagues, who were kind and happy for me, though they didn't understand. Ro and I got on the road to Albany in the middle of the afternoon of June 1st. The evening was fraught with pouring rain through an East Coast storm that seemed to follow us north as we drove up I-95. Through the dark rain we grumbled at each other, largely because of my personal displeasure at our later than anticipated departure for Maryland. After a tense six-hour drive, we arrived in Albany, New York, having made only one or two wrong turns along the way. The plan was to meet up with our hosts the Millers at a downtown Albany bar where a U2 tribute band called The Unforgettable Fire was playing in anticipation of the show tomorrow night. As we arrived in Albany, the bright edges of reality re-emerged to sharpen every moment, as my senses re-awoke to adventure.

The evening passed pleasantly enough, and the cover band was very good, but we were tired, and we left the bar early for the Miller homestead. We were informed that the house was unlocked and that we could enter freely to find our room on the first floor, marked by a sign with our names on it.

We found a charming house back winding country roads with a Beautiful Day Barbecue sign marking the gate. We parked my U2-mobile behind a car with the license plate "Love U2," stepped quietly past the darkened tents lined up in the backyard, and found our room inside the house. We planned to get up at a decent hour in the morning to stake our claim in line.

The next morning, we awoke to sounds of giddy laughter coming from the kitchen. Generally grumpy in the morning, I found myself confused by my own sense of well-being. Ro and I got up from the full-size futon that had been so hospitably allowed us and went out to explore the scene. It's a strange feeling waking up in the home of a kind stranger in Albany NY. It reminded me a bit of the extended family reunions of my childhood; the feeling of misplacement and an awareness of the nearness of virtual strangers, mixed with a vague anticipation of good things to come.

We joined a table of about six people and were generously served a hot breakfast. We learned that others had risen earlier and had left hours before to get in line for tonight's show, while Ro and I had been still snoozing.

The conversation flowed easily over breakfast. Allison Miller put us at ease quickly with her happy chatter and frequent giggles. Allison was eight months pregnant. Because of the pregnancy she and her husband Chris had been unable to plan to attend more than perhaps two shows. So, Allison explained, "We decided to bring the party to us!" This made perfect sense and I thought it was great that they had been able to make the best of a case of bad timing. Allison laughed as she jokingly scolded the band for not checking with her before setting the tour dates.

Ro and I finished breakfast and started getting things together quickly for a day of camping out at the Pepsi Center. Following my experiences of unpreparedness last month, we had packed quite a load of goodies and were well armed for many days of waiting in line. Our stash included a pair of fold-up camping chairs, a backpack full of toys like crossword puzzles, camera, novels, and my fan signature book. We also brought a cooler, which the Millers stuffed with barbecue food before we headed out the door.

We drove into the city of Albany and searched for tonight's venue. Winding through steep city roads, Ro got us to the Pepsi Center easily and we were very surprised to find the GA line looking rather long already at

10:00 a.m. I hopped out of the car and asked the queuers which end of the line was the front. They pointed me in the right direction and then informed me that I should go see the guy at the front of the line to get a number.

I had heard about the numbering practice while I tracked the tour online during my short break from following in person. The lines had begun to grow long earlier and earlier, and the fans had organized a simple system to police themselves. This involved some work on the part of the first people who got there, in the form of setting up a list of names and numbering everyone's hand with a marker as soon as they got to the venue to wait. The people who got there first were willing to do it because they had the most invested in maintaining the integrity of the line. It was a good idea that had arisen spontaneously from the group. This practice had seemed to help at other venues, although the venue security would have nothing to do with it and would not try to help enforce the fans' numbering system. They must have thought we were incredible geeks.

I got my number, 191, from the fans in front who reported they had been camping since about 2:00 a.m. They were alternately sleeping and rotating number duty amongst them. They were nicely set up in sleeping bags with the radio softly playing U2 Live at Red Rocks. I walked down the line, checking everyone out, and squatted at the end. Ro circled the block in the car and came back to find me and dump out all the previously mentioned goodies. He drove away past waves and exclamations from the line because I had painted in blue and purple my rear window with the words "The Goal is Elevation!"

I began setting up camp behind numbers 189 and 190. It was going to be a long day. It was 10:00 a.m. and U2 wouldn't hit the stage for almost 12 hours. Still, I wouldn't have been anywhere else right then. I settled into my camping chair with the cooler to my right and a crossword puzzle book in hand.

Before long, a group of five guys set up shop behind me in the line. I thought I had come prepared, but they did me one better. They set up a mini grill and started tossing cans of beer around to each other and anyone near us in line that wanted one. They had the right idea, and I settled in for an early summer barbecue as we awaited another incredible show.

The day passed slowly in a bizarre mix of nervous anticipation and contented boredom. The line behind me grew and soon had to wrap around and double back on the other side of the street lest it end up in a damp back alley. This created much concern about the possibility of a mad rush towards the door at show time, which might destroy the integrity of the now orderly queue. The people from the front kept numbering and after a little nervous speculation, we had to accept that we couldn't do better but to hope that our numbers would stand strong.

As the hours passed into a warm midsummer afternoon, and more GA ticket holders showed up, the end of the line disappeared around the corner. U2 music sounded off and on through the day up and down the line. People slept, played cards, and watched each other. One gentleman walked up and down the line wrapped in a white sheet marked with a giant U2 in black across his back and collected the thoughts of whomever would sign it for him. An older lady and her son came over and chatted with us. She seemed rather eccentric, and Ro and I immediately dubbed her The Bird Lady. One of the guys next to us had matching tattoos on the backs of his ankles with a U on the left and a 2 on the right. As the crowd grew, I spotted Christian and Mike walking down the middle of the cobblestone street and chatting to each other as they surveyed the line. I pointed my friends out to Ro and shouted out my hellos to them. They stopped as they passed our position in line and greeted us warmly.

I felt I was home again!

Around 2:00 p.m. I left Ro at camp and took a walk to observe what was becoming of the rest of the line behind us. I found people curving up and down around the building across the street from us. The fans in front had stopped numbering at 300 from which point the line continued, numberless. I felt quite happy then to be the proud bearer of 191 on my right wrist.

The afternoon passed slowly, with many crossword puzzles partially completed, several new signatures added to my fan book by the BBQ guys next to us, and a photo of myself taken with these nice boys. We enjoyed the afternoon together and the warm mutual acceptance that comes easily to those who share a strong passion. Unfortunately, the relaxed anticipation that we shared was to be destroyed in a moment of panic when the line surged forward in an avalanche of gathering movement. I saw a bit of a shift up front, and the next thing I knew we were all running, RUNNING, forward to God knew where. An attempt to save my camp was short-lived. As I struggled with chairs and cooler (Ro had gone in search of a bathroom and missed the melee), I saw one after another queuer from behind pass me by. No, this would not do. I ditched my worldly possessions and ran up to find the five guys who had been encamped behind me. Soon, we came to a dead stop behind a wall of people, and what had been a well-spaced, comfortable crowd of fans lounging the day away became a 10-deep mass of sweaty, standing people. Cranky people. The mood of the line had been punctured palpably by this pointless herding forward. Suddenly, people (including myself) were antsy, grumpy, and tired. We glanced at each other's numbered hands and realized we were hopelessly mixed up. Some even tried to straighten it out, but there was no way anyone was going to move anywhere.

I stood in my new unpleasant position and searched for Ro. To my great relief, he showed up and observed our new waiting position with dismay. It was only 4:30 p.m., two more hours until doors would open.

We all tried to make the best of a bad situation, and after what seemed like days, 6:30 p.m. rolled around and the line began to move again. Then began the ritual of obtaining wristbands and walk running as fast as you could to claim your station on the floor near the point's tip or in the heart. I tried to grab some rail near the tip of the heart, but the roomy allure of the enclosure drew me in. I had not been able to get an actual piece of rail and I didn't have the energy after the day's festivities and frustrations to accept the thought of the next four hours on my feet. So, Ro and I checked into the heart, which was fast filling up.

With our heart wristbands secured, we crashed out on the cement floor towards the back of the enclosed area. We needed a little rest, so that we could get our second wind. This heart was starting to feel homey, as I looked around and saw friendly familiar faces from my May trip. I caught up with Mike and Christian who were chilling in a circle of friends nearby. We waved to our barbecue friends who had claimed some floor outside the heart near the tip. Ro and I drank a couple of beers and waited for the show to start. PJ came on, and I could feel that her performance was growing on me. The sweet, skunky smell of marijuana floated over the crowd. I began to let go of the fatigue and anxiety that permeated the long day.

Once the concert started, Bono mentioned early in the evening that he was feeling ill, or as he put it, "totally fucked up," and told us the show was ours to carry. After a handful of songs, which I rather mellowly enjoyed from the rear portion of the heart on Edge's side, I wanted to get closer to the human forms of U2 (perhaps to minister to our ailing Bono myself?). I gently tried to push up through the crowd, but the closer to the front I got, the less people would be moved. I only got so far, and from there I could see mostly just the backs of heads. I soon retreated, feeling the need to dance as the song "Gone" ripped through the air and shocked its way through my body.

"Gone," that relatively unknown raging rocker from the Pop CD. To this day, every time I hear it, whether I'm hearing it live, in my car's tiny CD player, or on the Elevation DVD, I find my physical form literally taken over. My body moves to the pounding drum and bass as if my muscles are wired directly to the instruments, instead of my own brain. I had to move backward through the crowd so that I wouldn't hit anyone with an arm flying of its own volition. Edge's guitar solo took the crowd over from its first screaming note. We became a mass of fluid movement, one wave of humanity rocking together to this groove. You must realize that, at the time, I was unaware of this phenomenon of fluid rocking motion that moved through me, and all around me. I couldn't have told you about it at the time because I was a part of it. The droplet of water is unaware of the great crests of the ocean of which it is a part. I can only describe it in retrospect.

I stopped and listened as the singer broke into the bridge of the song and sang words that hinted of danger and temptation. Then the song slammed back into the chorus, and with those transcendent lyrics, we all let go together and the elevation began as the colors of the big screens behind the band, and Bono's heroic face, and the notes of Edge's ending guitar solo ripping into new heights, overtook us. I was lost in a musical universe of color, sound, and emotion as the song came to its completion. I lost myself in the moment. I knew not where I began and where the colors ended. I thought not of my separation from the people surrounding me that I did not know. I took the stimuli into myself, and I felt the joy of my deepest feelings, those that I didn't even understand, being expressed by an external voice that we all understood. As soon as I became aware that the boundaries between myself and the universe were merging, I was once again a separate being. Then I forgot that awareness as another blast of Technicolor and sound flooded my field of sensation. Again, I became one with moment.

This cycle of remembering and forgetting myself continued throughout the climactic end of "Gone." When the lights and guitar went out before the next song began, I caught myself and wondered what the hell had just been happening to me.

I didn't know what to call it then, but I do now. That was my first time at a U2 show to experience satori. According to Alan Watts, satori is "the experience of waking to our original inseparability with the universe." This is not some sort of intellectual idea; it is an *experience* of awakening. It is not something that can be grasped on a purely mental level. Satori comes like grace at times when one is profoundly open to it, and only at times when one is not actively seeking it. It happens for you…or it doesn't.

Although it may have been the first time that I awoke to this awareness at a U2 concert, it was not my first experience of satori. This awareness had visited me once, a couple of years prior during a six-month period during which I took up the practice of yoga and meditation just after my college years. Sitting in a modified lotus position at the end of yoga practice, as I focused on my breathing, I had spontaneously become aware of my inherent oneness with the rest of creation. At the time I felt as if I was free falling through open space, because I had lost my sense of self. This sense of self, or ego, is what establishes one's feeling of isolation and separateness from the world. At that time, this first experience of satori had felt rather disorienting, and even a little bit frightening, as it occurred. But in the end, the residue of a moment's awareness created a profound sense of peace and well-being that had stayed with me for many days.

Throughout the tour up until the show in Albany on June 2nd, I had been opening up psychologically and spiritually to the beauty of the community that is brought together by the positive ideals expressed in U2's music. Slowly but surely, I felt my awareness expanding. I believe that I was finally able to let go of my worries and anxieties, my false self/ego, in Albany on that night. The result was satori.

"New York," that dark-edged ode to the city, was next. Of course, this crowd of New Yorkers lost their mind when Bono crooned, "I just got a place in New York." The energy level went through the roof. Elevation was in full flight, thousands of passengers on this ship, and Bono had become for us a beloved captain.

There is something ritualistic and primitive about a rock concert at its peak of energy. The crowd is feeling so good, so pumped, and there is a need to focus the resultant feelings of awe and love onto an external being. Bono, of course, plays this role of "the worshipped one" to a tee. As U2 fans, we eat it up.

There is a reason that so many people let go of the fear of looking stupid, or naive, or even nerdy. If we're lucky, at least once in our lives we will each find a passion and go after it without letting anything get in the way, especially not worry about being misunderstood, or judged, or thought of as stupid. It's like falling in love. For U2 fans, the culmination of this passion comes in the form of a U2 concert.

Bono described something akin to this idea in a 1992 radio show called Zoo Radio, during a mock interview with BP Fallon:

BP: What does it feel like to be onstage, in front of so many fans?

Bono: Oh…it's high…it's incredibly high.

BP: How high is it?

Bono: It's…it's very high.

BP: Higher than making love?

Bono: It is making love.

One of the reasons that people who are in love choose to physically express that love is in the hopes of forging a stronger connection between them. This longing for connection can be mirrored in the rock show, as the fans reach out physically to touch the star, and a true rock star will reach back emotionally. A very good rock star will go ahead and make some form of physical contact, and Bono has carefully cultivated the art of being a very good rock star since the early 90s. So, it happened every night that the star would reach out physically to touch his fans, breaking down the symbolic division between worshipper and worshiped. Every time Bono did this, it was dramatic. Whether this sort of showmanship was dramatic in a sincere way or dramatic in a calculated way remains open for debate, though this writer (of course) tends to lean towards believing in Bono's sincerity.

On this night in Albany, the song "New York" began pulsing its way through the arena, and we caught our breath as the languid notes of the opening verse swam about us gently, yet insistently. Just as we felt our hearts slowing down to a tolerable beat, the band cranked it up to 70 mph and the audience was back on upward sense with the rising beat. Then, suddenly, the slow flow surrounded us again and Bono slinked his way out from the main stage along the catwalk. As we saw him begin to move, a small crowd of bodies began weaving in and out of each other in anticipation of getting within reaching distance as he passed on his way out to the tip of the heart. We gently but quickly swam through each other, never pushing, never rude, and those who chose to follow Bono's movements lined up behind the backs of the one-person-deep line that stuck to the inner heart's railings throughout the show. I stood behind a small girl and her small boyfriend about halfway back to the tip and waited.

As Bono continued to approach, eyeing the crowd on either side of him, the small girl was quickly hoisted on to her boyfriend's shoulders, and I slipped in on the railing where she had been. At almost the same instant, Bono's spotlight was spilling over the catwalk and down on to us. He slowed when he saw the girl smiling up at him. Security personnel followed Bono in the trenches around the stage, and they had been about to direct the girl to get down when it became clear that she had caught Bono's attention. Security backed off. Bono regarded this attractive fan as the music encircled us. He put one hand in front of his face, eyes covered like a blind man, and took a few stumbling steps towards her with the other hand reaching out in front of him, as if feeling his way through the dark. He halted, reached his fingers out to her, slowly, cautiously; he was teasing her, teasing all of us, as the fan stretched desperately for him. After an endless moment of anxious separation, during which the tips of their fingers were distanced from each other by decreasing inches, the audience let out a psychic sigh of relief as Bono allowed the girl to firmly clasped his hand into her own. They were joined physically for one powerful moment and then—the release. Bono let her hand go and continued moving down the catwalk.

He moved away and the girl hopped off her boyfriend shoulders. She hugged her boyfriend and I patted her warmly on the arm. "That was amazing!" I said with a laugh into her ear. She turned and grinned at me. I stepped back into the crowd, glowing. I felt as if I had just participated in a huge psychic love fest.

Dear Reader, please understand that I didn't mean it was amazing that Bono had grasped her hand. That would be mundane in any other context. What I found amazing was the powerful statement of unity between fan and band, on a symbolic level, and Bono's willingness to open himself to that.

As Bono had described a decade prior: a moment like this at a U2 show isn't higher than making love, it *is* making love.

The next two songs were old favorites, "I Will Follow" and "Sunday Bloody Sunday." Bono began to struggle vocally, clearly handicapped by his cold. It was becoming more obvious to the audience that the man was not in top form. During "I Will Follow," he improvised a bit of rap asking for our support:

Feelin' ill, feelin' low

So you're gonna carry the show

Gonna show Bono where to go

A short time later, Bono and Edge were at the heart's tip for a brief acoustic set. Tonight's version of "Stay" was particularly heartrending due to the woeful fight Bono was having with his voice. "Stay" is a powerful ballad with some powerful notes and poor Bono just wasn't quite up to it. The painful rasping sounds of his wail this evening made it the most poignant version of the song I had ever heard. I wept quietly as the song went through me. This song, too, seemed to be an expression of the contents of my own heart: if only I could stay at the shows, could they somehow be enough?

Bono's voice continued to slip throughout the remainder of the evening, and we in the audience did our best to help him out. The Albany crowd sang along lustily. By the time the show was nearing its end, Bono's voice was barely more than a whisper. Before the concert ended, he gave the crowd and the band his thanks. He told us that we had lifted him up out of his physical discomfort, and that he had had a great evening.

It felt pretty good to be able to give something back.

As Ro and I climbed back into the U2-mobile after the show, a concert attendee saw my rear window painted with the words "The Goal is Elevation." This kindred spirit shouted out from his vehicle as we sat in traffic, "Did you reach your goal tonight?" he asked me. "Hell yeah, I did!" I replied joyfully.

My spirit soared all the way back to the Miller homestead, where fans crashed out everywhere in search of some physical renewal before another show scheduled an hour's drive away in Hartford CT tomorrow night.

I woke after nine hours of coma-like sleep. I opened my eyes to another beautiful day, although it was raining in Albany. Ro and I joined the Millers for a lovely breakfast and quiet conversation. The Millers had an adorable little girl who repeatedly sang a tot's version of the opening chorus of "Elevation." Every time she yelped out, "MOLE in a HOLE! El-vation!" the small crowd around the table laughed and smiled at her. We exchanged plans for tonight's show, and it soon was time for Ro and me to hit the road for the GA line in Hartford. I was a little worried because it was getting late into the morning, and a good portion of the campers from last night had already vacated the premises for the Civic Arena. We took some pictures with the Millers and other guests, and I gave our hosts a handmade heart in a suitcase U2 pin that another fan friend had mailed to me months ago, after a brief meeting of the minds online. I asked them to pass it on to another U2 spirit who would appreciate it someday.

Ro and I got on our way after hugs and goodbyes were satisfactorily exchanged. I was awash with the residue of love and satori from the previous night's show. My heart hurt a little as we broke out of the warm haven that the Millers had provided. It would be hotels from here on out for Ro and me. During the drive, we tossed around ideas for a poster that I planned to construct for Bono tonight. Something like a get-well card, maybe. In the residual afterglow of all I had experienced emotionally and spiritually last night, I was completely smitten. I was overtaken with the need to direct this powerful love energy on to an external object. It was unwilling to admit it to myself, but I was totally absorbed in the hopes of personally communicating with our hero, King B, himself.

You could perhaps say that I had kind of lost the plot.

We drove into our next city stop around noon and followed signs to the Hartford arena for Ro's third chance to get elevated and my ninth stop on the tour. We found the downtown area and followed signs that took us into an underground garage. We parked, grabbed our supplies (cooler and chairs had been retrieved by Ro and taken back to the vehicle during that interminable two hours in line yesterday after I had ditched them). Today, I brought along my art supplies too. I had a little message to construct.

The Hartford arena was entered into by way of a mall, which sat attached like a barnacle to the giant rock of a gathering place. This meant that Ro and I would sit waiting inside an air-conditioned building today. To our relief, the line was much shorter at 2:00 p.m., quieter, and better contained, than it had been in Albany yesterday. Seated ticketholders quietly lined the walls of the small atrium, curving past shop fronts, which were closed and gated on this Sunday, June 3rd. We got numbers 120 and

121 marked on our wrists (different city, different fans taking names, same plan) and took our spot at the end of the line.

We immediately spotted Bird Lady, whom we had met yesterday, about thirty people ahead of us in line. I scoured the line for familiar faces but didn't spot any others right away. That's alright, more friends to be made, I thought cheerfully to myself. We settled in for another afternoon of waiting, and I pulled out my notebook to work out some sign ideas. I consulted with Ro on the proper wording:

Bono, hope you're feeling better!—

Booooring...

Bono, I saw you were sick last night, wanna play Doctor?—

NO...!

Bono, can I take your temperature? Hope you feel better! -

No...

Feeling frustrated, some ideas involving the concept of a "Nurse Marcy" came about.

Next thing I knew, I was working on a poster that read:

Bono, I saw you were sick in Albany last night...let Nurse Marcy heal you!

Might as well go for it, I figured. Ro was slightly confused by my behavior, saying, "But I thought you weren't *trying* to get on stage again!" Yeah, well, so did I.

The sign was constructed, and there were four men in line ahead of us who began chatting with me as I created my newest masterpiece on a modest piece of poster board. I found myself again settling into that comfortable sense of understanding, the fan-to-fan relationship phenomena which I had experienced innumerable times over the past three months. I was getting quite accustomed to it, and I explained my plan to my new friends. We joked about the whole thing, laughing as I penciled out the words "Nurse Marcy." The two nearest me, Jeff and Steve, came up with a new idea for the plan to get Bono's attention tonight...including actual nursing supplies and nursing costume. I thought this had some real potential, so I encouraged them to delve into my craft supplies and work on a nurse's hat. I had been half kidding, but to my amazement and delight, these four men put their heads together and worked out a design to make a hat out of my crude materials.

I continued coloring my poster as Steve and Jeff argued about the appropriate shape for a nurse's hat and how to best replicate it. Soon my new friends were amusing themselves by cutting, pasting, and even coloring a red cross on the front of their creation. I lent them my head for a fitting and was soon the proud bearer of a sign with an offer of healing and matching props. Some pictures were taken, and I passed my fan book around to my new compadres. Steve charmed me with a poem be fitting the occasion:

"Hartford...

Life, love, soul

Elevation is the goal

In an abandoned mall in an abandoned town

We helped to construct Nurse Marcy's crown!"

Fun was in the air, but it was darkened a little bit by the presence of an old friend of mine that threatened to ruin the whole thing. Who else, but ego?

The show last night had so knocked me off my feet that I was full of desire to personally express my appreciation to our star. Not only that, but I thought maybe I could do it. At the time, I was vaguely aware, but did not really care, that ego was leading me down this path.

I don't know if I can write about this. It's so hard to admit to. But I must try because the silly immaturity, while not pretty, is part of this story.

So, we were herded again into the arena, I with my hat and poster. I found a spot in the heart at dead center stage, behind just two rows of people standing together, packed like sardines. I was only about five feet from the front of the mainstage where Bono would stand in a few hours' time. I stood in the middle of a small crowd of happy, excited fans, and we talked and laughed as the minutes to show time ticked by. I met lots of fans, one of whom was a guy named Sean who had a tattoo of the Joshua tree on his shoulder that matched my own tattoo of the same, on my lower back. We all saved each other's spots for beer and bathroom runs and partied as we waited.

On cue, at 7:30, the lights went down for the opening band. PJ Harvey was glorious that night. She stood before us, a powerful yet lithe beauty with the hard voice of an angel. We admired her band and their music. Someone shouted out to her, "We love you, Polly!" and she smiled shyly and gave soft thanks into the microphone. We in the front jumped to her hard rocking set list, and I was wowed by one of the final songs she sang for us, called "Is This Love?"

I asked myself that very question as I adjusted my nurse's hat.

The house lights came up again after PJ and her band exited the stage. Pre-show music blared from the sound system, and we danced in the heart, and waved to the lighting workers who danced with us, as best they could, from their spots high above us in chairs hanging from the lighting equipment. The arena filled up quickly as I blew up balloons and batted them backward into the crowd. Most of them ended up on stage, and U2's crew was only moderately enthusiastic about batting them back. We shouted at Dallas, Edge's guitar tech, to send us back our toys and he obliged once or twice, teasing us. Willie Williams, the lighting director, checked the set up as we neared show time. He hurriedly, though good humoredly, reacted to the fans who cried out "WILLIE!" by turning and shouting back, "What?!" Used to being ignored, this shut the fans up.

The recorded songs that immediately preceded the show were carefully chosen and fans that followed were starting to recognize them. We knew it meant that U2 would be on momentarily when we heard the words to the old Jackie Wilson song, "Higher and Higher." We got lost in happy anticipation as we danced, waiting for the show to begin, enjoying this moment as much as any moment that we might experience during U2's time onstage. When Stevie Wonder's "Higher Ground" came on, that was the final sign. We knew that as soon as the three minutes of this song were up, the opening chords of "Elevation" would rise through the arena with the house lights still on.

I took one more look around the huge room at the thousands gathered and lined up in their spots near to and far from central stage. U2 joined us then, filing one by one on to the stage to the sound of roaring cheers as the opening lyrics echoed from Bono's mouth through the chamber. Then Bono was five feet in front of me, kicking it higher, and once again we were jumping. I held up my sign, but not all the way, because I didn't want to block the dozens of fans lined up directly behind me. Bono was so close to us I could have shoved it in his face. When the lights went down, the girl next to me suggested I hold up the sign higher, so I did. Someone tapped me on the back and said, not unkindly, "You're blocking a lot of people behind us."

Doh! I lowered the sign a little.

Then Song Two, "Beautiful Day" started, and as usual, Bono bent close and reached out towards us as he sang the lyrics inviting us to touch him.

As Bono leaned forward into the crowd, teasing us, his adored face was not more than two feet from where I stood. I lifted the sign through a dozen reaching fan hands for one last time up to Bono's eye level for him to read it. Unfortunately, the only reaction from our hero was a flicker of confusion across his face (or was that irritation?), and more to the point, someone behind me batted it right back down and it went to the floor. "Put it back up!" Ro prodded me.

"No, I can't, it's blocking people!" I yelled back. Also, I'm starting to feel like a real asshole, I thought to myself. I grabbed the poster from the floor and stood there, feeling small. I was rather confused by this feeling of smallness. It was such a marked contrast to what I was used to feeling at U2 concerts, that was, a heavenly elation. After a few more songs passed, my confusion (and was that... hurt?) drove me away from the crush of the front and I sought open spaces toward the back of the heart, still clinging to the idea that maybe I could hold the sign up back there and Bono would be able to see it better during one of his trips around the catwalk.

After that, I don't remember much about the Hartford show other than a depressing sense of removal from the whole event. This feeling was diametrically opposed to what I had felt throughout the previous night's show in Albany. I saw Bono through jaded eyes, and his performance tonight seemed less engaged, and less engaging, than it had been in Albany. His voice seemed a little bit improved, and he did make mention of the phenomenon that had happened to him, that is, being lifted up by the crowd last night in Albany. Tonight, I was painfully disappointed because I just couldn't get into it. It seemed that I was perhaps the only one who felt this way, as people all around me repeated the rite of celebration and love. I amusedly, removedly, observed the phenomenon of Bono followers repeat itself, as at least a dozen fans weaved through the crowd in the rear of the heart to follow the star's movements. During the celebratory intro to "Streets," one guy in the heart was so overwhelmed that he made his way down the line along the inner railing, giving high fives, hugging strangers, and clapping people on the shoulder, all of whom grinned back at him. I wanted to participate but felt left out, and I had some idea of why.

Ego had reared its ugly head. I had allowed myself to get so carried away that I felt as if I had the power to control Bono's actions (*Yeah sure, I can make him pull me up with him, it worked before! Not once, but twice!*

My, was I getting greedy). Plus, I went so far as to block other fans' clear view of the stage to meet this end; essentially, I put my own ambition before the collective wishes of the group (and they put me in my place for it, by batting my sign down—good for them!) When it didn't work out the way I wanted it to, for the sole pleasure and gratification of myself, I was trapped in a sulky state like a little kid. I came back to earth with a thud as I realized that I had, in fact, lost the plot. I went in there with expectations that I had no right to harbor, and as a result the show was ruined for me. I let my poster slip to the concrete floor amid crushed beer cups and sheepishly put my nurse's hat in my back pocket. I tried to enjoy the rest of the show but couldn't get beyond myself. Besides that, my fatigue was catching up with me. This created a wall of physical, spiritual, and emotional discomfort that I couldn't penetrate to take part in the moment.

There was no experience of satori that night, but the self-inflicted slap in the face did bring me back to reality. As we filed out of the show, Ro and I talked it over. The concert from his perspective was more in line with what I had experienced last night: a great time. This reinforced what I was afraid of—my sense of removal and my perception of Bono's performance as being contrived was born out of my own head trip. Ro and I found a bar and had a seat for a post-concert beer. U2 music was playing as usual, and I started feeling slightly over-saturated with the thing. I sat moping and noticed the guy to my right. We struck up a conversation about the show. I even shared with him the rather embarrassing process and resultant lousy feelings that I had and still was experiencing this evening. He signed my fan book with some words that helped me to put it in perspective:

Hartford, June 3rd 11:55pm

U2 is an experience!... A U2 show culminates when you look at the person next to you and infectiously smile for no reason. And for a brief moment, everyone in the arena is one with the music and each other.

These words gave me comfort and reminded me what it was all about. I hadn't spent all this time and energy for the end goal of personal contact with Bono, or any of the individual members of U2. I was doing it because of the music and the community that it had given birth to, and the love that was being generated, every single night that they took the stage. I was relieved to realize that now, after becoming aware of what I had gone through here and why, I could almost certainly be a part of the U2 experience again: if only I could leave this behind.

We woke the next morning to the luxury of a day off. Slowly we began moving and we didn't get out of Hartford until around 3:00 o'clock in the afternoon. Entering Massachusetts, we found a welcome center where we stopped to get some info. We had plans to be in Boston for the next three days and nights and hoped to find some time for a little sightseeing. I booked the cheapest room I could find, about fifteen miles out of city center, and we hopped back in the car to drive the last stretch.

As we drove, I told Ro that I had realized something rather bittersweet last night in Hartford. It was something from the song "Kite," a wistful ballad from the new CD. I had never been terribly fond of this song, but it spoke to me last night and I would never hear the lyrics in the same way again.

The song is, in Bono's words, about "letting go of someone you're not ready to let go of." I had heard this rather obvious explanation from him before and it all seemed rather basic and uninteresting (maybe this is because I've never really lost anyone close to me, thank God). But at last night's show, I heard these words as if it was the ideal of "Bono" (that image created by my own mind) that was singing the song to me. I mean, really, I had been idolizing this band since I was fifteen years old, nine years ago. I had used U2 music to escape long before I ever became acquainted with drugs or alcohol. U2 music had helped me express myself as a teen, and it soothed my acute sense of isolation and loneliness when I was less mature. So maybe I needed to hear, in the real Bono's voice, the words of my imagined, idealistic, comforting Bono, telling me that I did not need him anymore. Telling me gently to grow up. Letting me know that I finally could.

After working all this out in communication with Ro, he turned to me and said, "I was hoping you would get that very message." It's amazing how someone who loves you can see how you might grow before you see it yourself.

I resolved to myself that I would go into these last shows of my tour, over the next two weeks, with a more grounded approach to what I was doing and why. I refocused my energy on enjoying the moment, the community, and the phenomena of the U2 concert for what it was.

That night, after checking into our hotel, we decided to go into the city to have a gander. We went on a little reconnaissance mission to Boston's Fleet Center, which would be home to the next four U2 concerts (all, of course, sold out). At 11:30 PM on June 4th I was rather surprised to find a clump of about a dozen fans already forming a line, complete with numbered name list. After chatting for a few minutes with these hardy folks who stood wrapped in their sleeping bags, I rejoined Ro in the U2-mobile, and gave him the report. We decided we'd better get back to the hotel, catch some shut eye, and hop right back up here to get in line at dawn. We had a bit of extra motivation to get as far up in line as possible for this show... it was rumored that U2's video producer, Dreamchaser Productions, would be taping the first two shows in Boston for an HBO special. Ro and I hoped to grab our spots along the rail and join the fans in the annals of U2 videography tomorrow night.

As I lay down to sleep that night, I pondered more on "Kite's" lyrical themes of mortality and living life to the fullest. I felt in my heart that this was the real reason I was doing this. No regrets. No missed opportunities. No matter how this crazy adventure would turn out for me; afterwards, I knew that I would feel like I had lived.

I woke reluctantly from a dreaming slumber just a few hours after we had retired to welcome the dawning day of June 5th. I dragged my fatigued body into a cold shower, which woke me physically, though not quite mentally. Ro drove us back down to the Feet Center. We arrived still groggy and took in the familiar scene of the GA line as scheduled, at 5:00 AM. It's funny how things can change; only a month prior in Pittsburgh I had thought that getting in line at 8:00 AM seemed a little nutty. But the tour had been on the road long enough, and U2 fans are such a community of information exchange, and people idolized this band so much, that people had started showing up earlier and earlier to line up for the show, always in the hopes of getting as close as possible to our somewhat reluctant heroes. Also, we were learning to look at the process of the GA line as a part of the whole experience. It gave us an excuse to hang out all day and discover new friends in each other.

Ro and I had our hands marked with numbers 54 and 55 after being dutifully entered in the logbook by our friends whom we had met five hours ago, before sleep. I sat at the end of the queue and set up camp while Ro went to forage for coffee and egg sandwiches. It was a chilly Boston morning before dawn, and I burrowed under a thin blanket that we had brought along. The sky stretched over me, hazy and gray, lit only with glowing predawn light. I sleepily looked at the line. No familiar faces, but lots of friendly ones. Four Canadian girls showed up and got numbers, then immediately asked if it was cool if they left for several hours then returned later. I advised them not to stay gone too long because I had no idea what was going to happen to this line over the course of the next thirteen hours. After they had checked out, a young guy with glasses and his little blonde buddy sat down to my left. They looked to be about nineteen or twenty years old. We struck up a conversation and the guy with glasses (let's call him Chuck) showed me some decent photos he had taken at other shows. I noticed that his little blonde buddy (let's call him Buddy) was quietly shivering to himself, and I gave him an extra flannel I had brought. He accepted it but seemed surprised that a perfect stranger would give him a shirt to wear. Chuck explained to me that this was Buddy's first U2 show and so I knew that he simply wasn't accustomed to the kind of warmth and spirit of sharing that tended to permeate these events.

Buddy wore my shirt for the next several hours, and I was glad not to see him shivering anymore. These guys immediately started feeling vaguely like the little brothers I never had. Ro returned with coffee and breakfast sandwiches, and I introduced him to our neighbors for the day. We settled in. The light grew and soon weak rays of sunshine crossed long across the concrete top of the underground parking deck next to the Fleet Center entrance. The city began to wake up as I tried, with no success, to doze off.

Bostonians on their way to catch the subway connected to the Fleet Center gave us quizzical stares as they went about beginning their routine Tuesday. Some stopped and asked what we were doing. After all, the site of about 100 people basically squatting on the Fleet Center's concrete sidewalks at 8:00 AM on a regular workday was a bit odd. We told them we were waiting for the U2 show tonight, and they nodded and smiled as they slowly backed away. I smiled quietly to myself, okay with the fact that these good normal people thought we must be crazy. The payoff of letting go at a U2 show was (and still is) well worth all the strange looks, head shakes, and lack of understanding from both strangers and those dearest to me.

Fleet Center security arrived at their posts around 8:00 AM. We listened carefully as the head of security spoke to the line. He explained that soon, we would move the line into a fenced off space on top of the adjacent parking lot. They were setting up temporary dividers like the ones at amusement parks used for managing lines that form for the newest rollercoaster. I was thrilled. With this system, the line would be strong and secured. At number 54, I was rather invested in my spot in line.

Soon thereafter, they moved us into the enclosure, and we set up camp again. It was still chilly, and we looked longingly at the sun's rays that approach slowly but surely as it rose in the clear morning sky. Soon we would be sitting in the warming light.

The day passed slowly and pleasantly enough, apart from the fatigue of sleep deprivation, which clung to my bones like moss. I received a call on the cell from my California friend Marcus, and he stopped by for a quick hello and hug. He had the reserved seating tickets for tonight, which I had swapped with him for the GA tickets that Ro and I would use tonight. Freed of the burden of waiting in line for today, he was spending a pleasant day hanging with his friend who lived in Boston. It was good to meet this man who had further shown me, a month earlier, the trusting and generous nature of the U2 community.

I amused myself for several more hours by working crossword puzzles, talking tour with the fans around me, and sharing my craft supply with the young couple next to me, who were working on posters for tonight's show. The girl colored one inviting Bono to dance with her, and the guy got creative with one meant to be a sort of congratulations card for Bono, whose wife had just given birth in the preceding weeks to their fourth child. The congrats poster was quite cleverly done with a baby bottle wrapped in a blue ribbon and a cigar wafting glittery smoke. I worked on my own little piece of artwork in the notebook that also served as my journal. I drew a picture of a kite set free to float on the breeze underlined by the lyrics to the song.

I was feeling a bit like a kite myself. The focus on my tour had shifted away from the band itself. I was coming into my own, and really feeling a sense of belonging stronger than I had ever experienced before, in the friends that I had found in the U2 community. My eyes were opening to all the beauty that U2's music often refers to. I felt the sheer wonder of being alive and meeting loving people, of encountering new adventures in each moment instead of constantly worrying about what may come tomorrow, or how I screwed up yesterday. The world seemed full of joyful possibilities. I was sucking the marrow out of these moments. I was not letting this beautiful day get away. I was not preoccupied with planning some sort of elaborate scheme to get Bono's attention because I had learned a bit of a lesson in acceptance and the danger of unreasonable expectations at Hartford's show two nights ago. I was simply immersed in what the moment had to offer. This focus on the moment, on receptiveness and acceptance, I now believe, opened me back up to the potential of another spiritual, even satori-esque, experience like what had happened in Albany. However, I wasn't thinking about satori (I wouldn't have even known what to call it anyway) at the time, which is good, because how can one achieve satori if one is hoping for it, that is, mentally grasping at it? One would be too busy hoping, and wanting, to lose oneself in the moment. It's much like the Zen idea that sitting and meditating may lead you to enlightenment, but wanting that enlightenment prevents its very occurrence. The mind must be clear, free of judgment, and receptive simply to what is.

My mind felt free as I colored a blue sky behind my elementary drawing of a kite, its tail flowing in the breeze, and drew vee-shaped birds flitting past a white fluffy cloud that I would line with silver glitter.

The hours continued to pass slowly, and the sun rose overhead until we were too hot on the concrete surface. Having learned a different kind of lesson in Pittsburgh, Ro and I slathered our bodies with SPF 35 sunscreen. The girls who had claimed numbers and left immediately this morning had reappeared late in the morning. Later in the afternoon, the girls and our other new friends Chuck and Buddy held our spots for us so we could go grab a bite to eat. We searched the surrounding neighborhood for a wrench and screwdriver so that we could pry my license plates off the car to take into the show. The best we could find was a set of children's toy tools at a local CVS. They did the job surprisingly well. I removed a shoelace from one of my inline skates stashed in the car's trunk, so that I could tie them to the plate and hang it around my neck during the show. Here we all were in U2OPIA, on tour with U2 after four years of waiting. I had to show off the plates. Also, I thought maybe I would spot the plate months later, on TV when the HBO special would be aired. I had seen numerous U2 plates on other concert videos.

By the time we got back to the line, over two hours had passed, folks were standing, and the whole group had shifted slightly forward. It was about 4:30 PM. Ro and I grabbed our pillows and lied down flat on our aching backs to wait some more. Lying down on the hard concrete felt luxurious. We had been out there for nearly twelve hours, and we were going on a poor night's sleep to begin with. Soon, it was time to pack up camp again and Ro hauled it back down to the car. I worried for the next 30 minutes until his return just as they were letting us into the Fleet Center in slow groups of about 25. The increased security and the methodical nature of the whole production was quite nice, and when Ro and I were at the beginning of the next group to be ushered inside, I thanked the security guy who had spoken to us ten hours ago. I told him I had been to lots of shows and no arena had done half as good a job as the Fleet Center was doing. He admitted it had a lot to do with the video production that was going on tonight and tomorrow night. Regardless, I hugged him and took a photo of him, my new favorite security guard, for my Elevation tour scrapbook.

It was our turn to enter the building. We were carefully ushered upstairs where we rejoined the line, which waited along the stairway as each fan, one by one, received their floor wristbands. We were all getting kind of goofy with fatigue and excitement by then. We joked around with the four Canadian girls behind us and shot more photos. There was a pair of women behind the girls who were holding rolled up posters. One of these women looked to be about twenty-two and was wearing a tastefully done belly dancer's outfit. I complemented her on the get up and asked if I could see her poster. She replied, "OK, but you're gonna hate me." She unraveled her poster and it read:

BONO, I SHOULD HAVE HUGGED YOU IN CHICAGO!

THANK U FOR THE DANCE!

THE BELLYDANCER

Ah-ha! I thought to myself, our on-stage belly dancer from Chicago!

"I don't hate you!" I gushed, "I saw that show! You did a great job!"

We grinned at each other, and I took yet another photo for the scrapbook.

After about a half hour of this preshow fun and excitement, we started moving up the stairs again. We were led through a door that opened into the still empty arena. There was a camera on rail tracks set up on the outside of the heart, and a more elaborate lighting setup. These alterations were obviously set up for the filming tonight. An abbreviated mad dash down the stairs through the $130 reserved seats began, to claim rail position. We received our heart wristbands on the way into the catwalk enclosure, and claimed a front row spot a little further from the center than I had hoped, on Adam's side. We could have gotten second or third row right in front of Bono's position, but I was unwilling to go the rest of the evening without a railing to lean on.

From our rail spots, we watched security and activities occurring on stage and throughout the arena. There were a lot more people working tonight, and many of them were wearing polo shirts marked with the Dreamchaser Productions logo. One of these people was standing right in front of us with the camera, and another man sat with his camera tucked into a corner near the rear of Adam's side of the stage. The one in front of us stood next to his assigned camera angle and watched the crowd looking disengaged. I asked him if he would be willing to take a shot of Ro and me. He obliged, still looking bored. When he passed the camera back, I asked if I could take a picture of him. That perked him up, and he smiled for a nice picture of the unnamed cameraman. I felt warmth inside that came from seeing someone smile, especially someone who had formerly looked so bored, or maybe even slightly annoyed. In that moment, positive energy bounced briefly in between us and grew. He smiles out from the pages of my scrapbook now, still anonymous.

After satisfactorily sussing out the situation, Ro and I plopped down on the base of the security fence to take a breather. We sat leaning against the fence and each other. Judging from the growing numbers of legs, shoes, and voices, I sensed the heart filling up. After about ten minutes or so, the sounds drew me out of my respite and I stood to look around as Ro took off to get us some beers and a pretzel, which would serve as dinner. The belly dancer chick saved his spot for him, and I chilled as I waited for his return. I was distracted by hunger.

I forgot my hunger and fatigue about fifteen minutes later, when the lights went down and PJ began her set onstage. She, as always, looked beautiful: lithe, shiny, and vibrant. Her music drew me in again tonight. I felt the pleasure of discovering another great rock band, especially in an artist that had really turned me off the first few times I had heard her. All five of the musicians in her band were worthy of admiration for their prowess, and I settled in to watch the Blonde Chick that stood in front of me playing various instruments (some of which I don't even have a name for). I had watched this Blonde Chick, admiring her talent, at the past few shows. She always stood in the shadows relative to Polly's glitter and glam rock star look. Blonde Chick wore all black every night in the form of a simple t-shirt and pants and pulled her hair back into a ponytail. I admired her seeming lack of desire or need to attract attention to herself as a sex symbol. Her talent stood on its own (not that PJ *needs* the sex symbol aspect, but as the lead vocalist, it doesn't hurt to have some). Blonde Chick seemed shy, not interacting much with the crowd, just focused on her playing. I had never seen her smile. I, the belly dancer, and a couple of dancing girls behind us got together during a break between songs and shouted: "We love you, Blonde Chick!"

Blonde Chick looked up quickly, grinning. We had brought her out of her shell! Another positive vibe exchange had been accomplished!

PJ's set ended, the lights came back up, and I wondered where the hell Ro was when he appeared, bearing gifts of beer and a giant pretzel. So nice! I wolfed down the pretzel in no time and we both finished our beers before too long. I decided to venture out to the concessions for round two. With the house lights on, and people fast filling every reserved seat, the mood in the arena was growing into something powerful. I took it all in as I followed the pathway out of the enclosed area. They had a small corridor set up for those of us in the heart to get most of the way back from the inner sanctum to the concessions, which were at the very back of the arena's floor for all the GA ticket holders. I felt somewhat self-consciously "VIP" as I walked from the front of the stage back through this corridor. I was wearing my plate around my neck and got a few waves and cheers as I passed. I waved back at all the shiny happy people.

I returned soon thereafter and was let through the security checkpoints as I held up my right wrist, which bore the heart wristband. Having gained admittance, I squeezed back through the fans that were now packed tightly around the stage, to my spot on the rail, and passed Ro his beer. The pre-show party continued in its fashion as we watched the roadies and light designers and Dreamchaser crew scurry about, and we listened to the familiar and still exciting pre-concert soundtrack. Balloons bounced around the heart as anticipation grew to fill the arena, and the smell of beer and marijuana wafted past. When we heard the familiar banging notes of Stevie Wonder's "Higher Ground," Ro and I took turns ducking down and taking quick puffs of our own joint, blowing it down and back into the crowd, away from the security personnel standing just a few feet in front of us. There wasn't much reason to worry about getting busted for a little joint if we weren't obvious about it. The smell was all over the place. When we emerged, Adam's roadie Stuart seemed to be making final adjustments to Adam's set up. I shouted out, "Hey Stuart!" and he looked at me, then leaned over towards me a little to hear me as I continued speaking to him. I hollered out as politely as possible, "If I wait here after the show do you think you could give me a set list?" He nodded at me. Then he was off into the underworld below the stage.

Soon thereafter, the show started, with no discernible difference from any other night: except that there was no one blocking my full clear view of the main stage. That was a first, and it immediately made the sixteen-hour-long wait worthwhile. I jumped up and down waving my U2OPIA plate overhead a great deal throughout the first song. I was trying to show it to U2, but Bono was not looking our way, Edge was clear on the other side of the stage, and Larry was hidden behind his drum kit as usual. However, Adam was soon smack in front of us, and my goofy behavior was rewarded with a huge grin and nod from our bassist hero when he took his place on stage and spotted my license plate. Hurray! Super positive energy exchange!

"Mysterious Ways" was played early in the set that night in Boston, and the belly dancer next to me started going a little crazy with waving her poster and jumping about. Ro had left my side to allow the smaller people behind him, including the belly dancer, have a better view. Ro is six foot one and considerate enough to step aside so that nearby people of smaller stature can see better. The belly dancer jumped, and I waved my arms and pointed down at her, on the off chance that Bono might look this way and his attention might be directed to the young woman with the poster meant for his eyes. I felt much better trying to help a younger girl get the man's attention, rather than futilely trying to catch his eye with my own sign, as I had been in Hartford two nights ago. Unfortunately, it did not seem that those piercing blue eyes were meant to gaze upon her, because there was no discernible acknowledgement from the worshipped one.

The concert proceeded as usual, and Ro and I kept our eyes on the mainstage throughout. Belly Dancer disappeared back into the heart's crowd, perhaps joining the small herd of nightly Bono followers. It was difficult to see much going on around the catwalk from this vantage point, and that was OK, because the show was so rehearsed, in a spontaneous looking way, that I knew exactly what was going on at the heart's tip as I listened to the music over the sound system. It was starting to dawn on me that…well, maybe U2 concerts aren't really designed to be seen more than a few times on the same tour.

I pushed these intrusive thoughts aside and allowed myself to be swept up in the show. I lost myself in the music and the crowd again that night. The emotional climax of these concerts came every night during the deep middle section of the show. By the time the show got to that point on June 5th, 2001, I was completely mesmerized by the music. I grabbed Ro and pulled him to me as the emotional, impassioned love ballad of "Stay" rang out through the arena. We held each other and swayed. I was already starting to lose track of myself as powerful emotion washed over me when "Stay" came to an end. Then, the beautiful segue leading into "Bad," when Bono led the crowd in a soft chorus of the classic concert closer of the 80s, called "40," after the Psalm of the same number. The crowd's chorus ended as Edge's guitar picked up on a new, quiet rhythm. I recognized the clear panging notes that are the intro to "Bad." Bono began singing over the soft cymbal strokes from Larry and the interlacing guitar chords. I continued to watch Adam, without thought, captive to the music and soft circling light and shadow that washed over the crowd behind the stage. I was in a place where I finally could let go...surrender...dislocate.

With this surrender came the freedom and absence of self-consciousness that allowed room for the kind of emotional catharsis that occurred next. Bono sang the next lines of the song as he rounded the top curve of the heart on Adam's side and walked in front of us back to his spot on center stage for the first chorus of "Bad." The passion of Bono's lyrical style, the faintly glowing light rays weaving through the back of the stage, and the perfect view I had of the entire band at this time was too much. I felt tears begin pouring down my cheeks, and I wrapped my arms around my shoulders in a self-hug. I was shaking a little from the chills, although I was at the same time sweating in the warmth of the dancing human mass.

Then, Bono begin to reach towards the crowd in front of him, and they all reached out to him, straining further, wanting to make contact so badly. As I watched the familiar drama unfold on the stage so close to me, there was still no thoughts, only emotion as the tears continued to seep from my eyes. Ultimately, I lost it, and my head dropped down into the cradle of my hands. I couldn't watch anymore, it seemed I was being overtaken until there was nothing left of me but poignant joy.

I held my forehead, and my shoulders shook with sobs as the song continued, and Edge was off into another guitar solo that somehow reflected both the anguish and wonder that set the tone of "Bad," supported by the pounding beat of Larry's drums and Adam's throbbing bass. They were one driving unit, and I was getting run over. I heard Bono crying out, "Not fade away! No no! Not fade away," then lead the audience in an exchange of "No's" over the band's force, which drove the song into a climax that ended in one last repetition of the chorus.

"Bad" never truly ended, there was no break in the flow of music. The song ebbed into the background, eventually fading out as I sensed the light changing and heard an organ's rising song. With this came one long lovely crooning sequence of notes from the voice, and the shimmering sound of guitar chords and individual notes being plucked. I lifted my head and looked up briefly. I was immediately confronted with the screens behind the stage glowing red and flashing successions of white as Bono let loose another crooning sequence of sound. Oh yes, I knew what was coming. My head fell right back into my hands, fresh tears pouring down.

When I was fifteen years old, I would watch the intro to "Where the Streets Have No Name" on my big brother's VHS cassette copy of "Rattle & Hum." It awed me then, in my longing to be close to the music and, yes, the creators of the music, I would dream of being there, live in concert, and soaking it all in. When I saw U2 for the first time at that tender age just once on the Zoo TV tour, I had been painfully disappointed by the physical distance between myself and the source of the music. Now, nearly a decade after that personally disappointing concert, I found myself in the very place of my adolescent dreams. The young girl woke in me as I stood there that night in Boston and wept in awe and gratitude.

Now, here in the year 2001, my case for adult emotional stability was weakened by the beginning of Bono's prayer, spoken over the rising intro to "Streets"—*what can I give back to God, for the blessings He has poured out on me?*—I didn't have a chance of composing myself, and I didn't give a rat's ass. I just kept listening with my head in my hands, crying, and shaking as "Streets" slammed into its bright beginning, and the crowd's roar grew and grew until it exploded in clapping, singing, and one great cheer as the house lights blazed on full blast. I couldn't look up as the lights blazed around me for perhaps a full minute. I felt as if I might explode if I were to look up.

Then it was dark again and I did look up as Bono pounded past us in a half-lap jog around the heart. I immediately found myself locking eyes with Adam Clayton, who may have noticed the hysterical female fan down front, and he smiled in amused benevolence down on my tear-streaked face. Phew...that brought me back to myself a bit and I looked around self-consciously, saying in Ro's ear, "Damn, I just totally lost it!" as if he might not have noticed. He put his arm around me and hugged me reassuringly. Having re-found myself, and feeling recentered, I was able to enjoy the rest of the song from an upright position, pogoing up and down with everyone else. "Streets" ended as "Pride" began, and then the band waved goodbye to go towel off before the first encore.

Too soon, the show's consistent closer, "Walk On," was upon us. I took one last shot at waving my license plate like a mad woman as I hopped around, joyfully participating in the final Hallelujah chorus. As usual, at the end of the show, U2 looked around and waved goodbye to everybody and shook a few fans hands. I strained forward, hoping to get a handshake from Adam, but had to be contented with another smile and a wave goodbye from him. A moment later, Adam met Bono between their spots on stage and Bono hugged his old friend. My gaze fell on Bono, and I lifted my license plate one more time. To my utter delight, Bono disengaged from Adam, turned those blue eyes in my direction, leaned over, and flashed a peace sign right at me. I returned the sentiment, thrilled beyond belief. Yay! They read my plate! They got *this* message!

Then the house lights were up, and soft music pumped through the sound system as folks filed out. Before I knew it, Stuart had emerged from the underworld and was peeling Adam's set list off the floor, which he then handed directly to me. He had remembered my request from hours ago. I was too thrilled to get anymore thrilled, so I just stayed thrilled for quite some time.

I was not able, or at least had no urge, to speak as Ro and I followed the crowd out of the arena. "Wow" was pretty much the only word that my brain was able to process at the time anyway. We popped out of the Fleet Center back to our former waiting spot. I saw Christian standing around watching the crowd, perhaps looking for someone.

"Christian! Oh my God! That was fucking amazing!" I gushed basic inanities such as these and Christian smiled the biggest, or perhaps only, smile that had graced his cool European features since I met him in Indy. I enveloped him in a markedly American bear hug, and he hugged me back. He said sedately, "Yes it was." We exchanged quick "see ya tomorrows" and Ro and I made a beeline for the car, passing a few fans already lined up for general admission in preparation for tomorrow night's show. Ro and I had reserved seats tomorrow, which would be a welcome break after three of the past four days spent in GA lines. We needed to rest up before tomorrow night's show.

Looking back, that day and night of June 5th at the Fleet Center was the peak of the tour for me. It just didn't get any better than that. It couldn't.

CHAPTER FOUR:
SEPARATION

After a lazy morning sleeping in at our hotel room, Ro and I rolled out of bed and headed back downtown with the intention of doing a little sightseeing. We ended up bumming around in the vicinity of the Fleet Center. We went to chat with the GA folk at about 3:00 PM and I ran into Mike and then Marcus. They were waiting separately in the line which had been cordoned off securely as it was yesterday. I introduced Mike and Marcus to each other, and they were kind enough to pose for a group shot with Ro and me, for my scrapbook. It came out great. We all look so happy. How could four strangers look so happy to be together? Well, because it was just another beautiful day in tour land.

Ro and I went down to the local Irish pub where U2 fans were already preshow partying. We spotted a woman whom we had met at the Millers house back in Albany and chatted with her while we quaffed a couple of pints. I grabbed the *Boston Globe* for the review of last night's show, which, to my surprise, dogged Bono's performance. The journalist described the singer's performance as below par, and not as strong as his bandmates. Yowch! That was a bit harsh, I thought. He sounded good to me, but perhaps that was just in relation to the raggedy voice we heard in Albany and Hartford.

A couple of hours later we headed back toward Fleet Center and found our seats in time to watch PJ Harvey. There was a somewhat hectic buzz about the place as we climbed to endless flights of stairs in the rear corner of the arena to watch the show again from a bird's eye perspective. It reminded me of our Chicago setup, and it was a good place to watch the final show in a week's string. It put it in perspective.

It was strange being up there. I watched the preshow party on the floor instead of being in it. I looked down on the ant-sized figures inside the heart and thought, damn, I was way down there last night. We had heard rumors that last night's show had served as the dress rehearsal to tonight's definitive taping of the show. This annoyed me slightly, but whatever. Last night hadn't felt like rehearsal to me. The other dynamic happening tonight was a live halftime broadcast to the NBA playoffs. Carter Alan, old friend of the band, and legendary DJ to first play U2 on American radio in 1980, was there. He warmed the crowd up a little, explaining that we were all going to be on national television! How exciting! Surely U2 was praying for a lively crowd tonight. This was the show that would live forever in our DVD players, for posterity's sake.

There were definite advantages to being up on top. After the show started, I was able to observe the light show again, the screens behind the stage, the flashing lights encircling the heart catwalk, and I was able to better appreciate the hugeness of the crowd. The show was great. Really great. Bono was back to his normal over-the-top self, as if to prove himself to that ornery *Globe* reporter. He even asked the crowd early in the show, "Am I singin' alright?" He was, of course, rewarded with a huge cheer. Bono also confirmed the rumor that last night was a dress rehearsal, saying smugly to the crowd, "Don't tell anyone, but we were just warming up last night." As if to show that he was indeed warmed up, Bono fully body-surfed the crowd in front during "Bad." He also pulled up a guitar playing member of the audience for an impromptu performance of "People Get Ready" to which he made up new words because he couldn't remember the original lyrics and threw a basketball in a giant arc over the heart for the benefit of the NBA at the appropriate time. Last but not least, he pulled a young woman up onstage during "With or Without You." He laid on the catwalk with her, watching the starry images floating across the arena ceiling. It was a great show, largely because there were some spontaneous moments.

I noticed a couple of strange things when the show started though. First, at the end of "Elevation," I clearly saw what appeared to be an empty spot down in the heart. It was strange... There were all kinds of fan heads bopping about, but then in the back on the right side there was a spot that was dark, and empty...a hole. I asked Ro if he saw it, but he didn't, so I forgot about it for the moment.

The other strange thing was that somehow Bono and the band got way off sync during "Kite." They basically had to skip a whole verse, which Bono then managed to tack on at the end. Also weird, but I was kind of glad because I figured now, they would have to use at least some footage from the first night. These thoughts disappeared as we enjoyed the last in a string of four great U2 shows.

There was a new prequel that started the near show's end performance of "The Fly":

The lights go down in the sports hall, it's a whole different scene

Light and motion, light and motion

Lights up emotion inside

It's hard to walk away

When you could have it all!

We could have it all!

But…

These words reflected all that I had been through in the past weeks.

During those days following the tour, as U2 fans we did have it all. We had each other, we had our music, and we were experiencing that elusive sense of freedom to follow our hearts and be true to ourselves. We had community, communion, and spiritual release. But…reality was knocking on the door, and all good things must come to an end. Even though I had three more shows slated for the following week, things were changing for me. This show was getting a bit tired. The repetitive setlist and Bono's practiced choreography, with moves that had looked so spontaneous the first time I had seen them, was starting to lose effect. Bono's rock star bit was starting to look like just that… a bit. The time was fast approaching to say goodbye, and I was somewhat fearful about what could fill that spiritual hole in my own heart, which had been satisfied by planning for and participating in the Elevation Tour over the first half of the year.

This tour's performance of "The Fly" was an expression of that need to move on in life, to find new dreams, even beyond love and adoration. Bono ran about the catwalk, casting suspicious looks over his shoulder at the fans reaching for him, playing a nervous sage who spouted strange and compelling bits of wisdom. The verse which called out artists as cannibals and poets as thieves spoke to me. I knew a little bit by this point about killing my inspiration with overconsumption. I did not know that a year later, I would be writing about my grief.

During "The Fly" Bono played the part of the paranoid, freaked-out idol to a tee. His demeanor during this song cried out, "Leave me be! What more do you want?" He sang about a character overwhelmed by showers of adoration while he personified the idea. Here was Bono running from the wall of love in epic proportions, a sheer volume of adoration that few human beings will ever experience. Then, Bono made a dramatic exit. As he sang the last lines, he tumbled down into the GA crowd and ran out of the auditorium through a rear door, flanked by security. I saw several fans in the rear GA area try to follow him out the door, but they were blocked.

How's that for risky? This move hadn't been utilized since much earlier in the tour, back in March and April. At that time, I had wondered how Bono could be so trusting of humanity (or was it just stupidity? as I had wondered in the case of Marcus, who sent his GA tickets cross-country to me with no guarantee on the return). Even with the bodyguards, someone down there might have been capable of hurting him. We are, after all, talking about a person who's been the target of death threats for his political activism. Maybe the action of diving into the crowd reflected an echo of the feeling that Bono used to discuss in the early 80s, about how silly he would feel being up on stage with all the other people down in the crowd, looking up at him on his pedestal. During the War Tour of '83 he took much greater risks and got in trouble with the band for it, stage diving, jumping off balconies and such, into the loving arms of his fans. If you've ever seen Live Aid, you'll know what I'm talking about—when Bono scaled the wall down from the huge stage at Wembley Stadium and totally screwed U2's set list plans for the performance, by spending time down there hugging fans, and inviting a couple of women on stage with him. At that time, Bono commented that he thought he totally blew it for them. As it turned out, the leap down from the platform to be with his fans was one of the defining moments of the event. Back then it was a powerful symbol of unity between the rock star and the fan. Moments like this still can be a statement in that way. However, on June 6th, at the Fleet Center, it came off to me as a rather contrived move made for the benefit of the camera, because Bono had engaged in this stunt during the early tour dates, then abandoned it for whatever reason, until the cameras were rolling.

The show ended in typical fashion. Ro and I decided to take this last opportunity before parting with the Elevation Tour to try to run into the band in person. We got directions from some diehard fans outside the arena to The Four Seasons, where U2 was staying this week. We drove down to the hotel in hopes that they might make an appearance and shake some hands, perhaps sign some autographs.

There were about twenty fans waiting when we got there, and we ran into the young guy with whom we had spent yesterday in line, the same one who had made the "Congrats on your new son" poster for King B. He had been in the heart again for tonight's festivities, and he had some disturbing information from down front for me. Apparently, there had been a bit of a fiasco in the GA line tonight, then subsequently, in the heart. He reported that Scott Nichols, U2's longtime head of security, had come out with a team of video production types and plucked a good 50 to 75 people from the rear portion of the GA line to come into the arena first, out of turn. Reportedly Scott had lied to the other fans in line, saying that they were just testing some camera shots, when they had faced questions from the fans who were being left outside. This did not turn out to be the case. The chosen few went into the arena early and got the prime spots around center stage and the tip of the heart. It was unknown why this action had been taken, but speculation held that the ones chosen had been chosen because they looked more energetic (which certainly makes sense if they had not been waiting on the concrete for umpteen hours), or even more offensively, because these fans would look better on camera from an aesthetic point of view. Once inside the arena, the fans who had been passed over and left behind sought answers from security milling around, and even from Paul McGuinness, but had reportedly been shrugged at by Mr. McGuinness, and told by Scott Nichols that his bosses had told him to lie. This fan told me that this turn of events had prompted over a dozen people to stage a mini protest when the show started, sitting down near the rear of the heart for the first couple of songs.

Aha! I thought, so that explains the hole in the heart that I saw earlier in the evening. I was troubled by this news. It was out of sync with U2's reputation for treating their fans fairly. The news didn't jive with the encounter I'd had with Paul McGuinness back in Columbus when he had asked us if security was treating the fans fairly. It was certainly a small thing, but this discourtesy spoke volumes of the reality of U2's removal from their diehard fans; that they would condone and allow a deception like this to happen. The implications were not lost on the diehards, according to my new friend, the protesters had been crying broken-heartedly and holding each other in a sort of vigil during "One." According to this fan's report, the sitting protest at the show's start had been noticed by the band, and the members of U2 (especially Bono and Larry) had responded with subtle anger at their fans' behavior. This distraction to the band members may have explained the uncharacteristic flub during "Kite," noted earlier. I was thanking fate that I had not been on the floor tonight to witness this small betrayal.

I mostly wanted to ask Paul McGuinness what happened. I wanted to hear U2's side of the story before I would completely give into disillusionment (or was it just reality that I was fighting?) But, not surprisingly, considering the bad vibes that had been generated, U2 did not grace us with their presence outside the hotel that night. The closest we got was Carter Alan, who came out and chatted briefly, and I couldn't bring myself to ask him if he knew what had happened. I was too confused, and he probably would have claimed ignorance anyway.

Ro and I talked it over on the way back to our hotel. Because he wasn't a totally committed fan, he didn't see what the big deal was. I, however, remained troubled, and I decided I would continue looking for a resolution to this report online when I got home.

When I did get home, I was ready to move forward and let the tour come to its necessary conclusion. However, in seeking the truth about what happened in Boston, I was confronted with more questions than answers. Reports from people online in Boston confirmed all that the informant had told me. Additionally, I found a bit that had since run in the *Boston Herald* reporting the incident in the GA line on June 6th. Anger was alive in the microcosm of the U2 world. The angry fans were largely dismissed by most of the online fan base, which countered that they had overreacted and were acting like brats. At the time, it seemed to me that the U2 devotees who had not been in Boston on June 6th were not willing to consider that our heroes had made a mistake, that is, that they were human.

In my growing disillusionment, I wrote in my journal on June 9th:

Reports are surfacing from Boston that U2's security directly lied to people who had been waiting all night and all day. And that their head of security told fans that he was told by his bosses to lie to the fans.

This is a serious breach of trust and respect. I wonder if the band would claim ignorance. Either way, it's a blow to the band's reputation for the diehard fans. Maybe they don't need us anymore. Maybe we don't need them anymore.

On Monday, June 11th, I got off work early still feeling confused and hurt over the events at the last U2 show I had attended, and somewhat ambivalent about driving the three hours to Philadelphia for that night's show. Despite this, I hopped back in the U2-mobile, not ready to let go yet, and bought the first pack of cigarettes that I had purchased in over six months. I thought it might make a good t-shirt:

"I went to fourteen U2 shows and all I got was this lousy nicotine habit!"

I arrived in Philadelphia at about 4:30 PM and found a long line wrapping around the First Union Center. As usual, I scanned the line for familiar faces, but spotted only Bird Lady. I grabbed some sidewalk at the line's end and waited. After a short while my dear friend Christian ambled by. I called out to him, and he stopped by to visit with me. He had bad news. I asked him if he had heard about Boston, and he informed me that he had been one of those down in the heart that had sat in quiet protest. He described the scene there in detail and was notably distressed by the events that had occurred. He shared with me an encounter that a good friend of his had reportedly had with Bono last night, during which she asked Bono what had happened at Boston, from his perspective. Christian passed along the secondhand details of their encounter, and ended his report by telling me, rather bitterly, that Bono seemed to have "completely lost it."

Christian looked completely broken-hearted, and my confusion turned into a heavy bitterness and resentment towards Bono, a man that I didn't even know. I embraced Christian, we found momentary comfort in each other, and then he was off.

I considered selling my ticket, and probably should have, but I was feeling small and selfish. So, I went into the show and pouted a great deal to myself though I stood surrounded by a multitude of happy fans. Although I got a great piece of rail along the inner tip of the heart, I stared stonily at Bono when he passed by for the first time.

Before the show tonight a female fan had been passing out bubbles to folks in the GA line. During "Until the End of the World," Bono and Edge passed by as they enacted their mock-fighting routine, and I pulled out the bubbles and started blowing them across the catwalk. The bubbles floated about Bono and Edge, causing what I thought was a cool effect. Unfortunately, the bubbles didn't just float innocuously, many of them ended up stuck to Bono and Edge for an instant before they popped.

This must have been rather irritating to the U2 members, because after the song ended, as Edge ran back to the main stage, Bono turned around and looked down at me. He yelled at me, "OKAY OKAY OKAY!!" Surprised to find myself staring into Bono's angry face as he stared back down at mine, I stupidly reached up to him, offering the bubbles in my hand. He turned his back and looked out to the crowd from the tip of the heart as the show continued.

I turned to the girl standing to my right and said, "Did he just yell at me?" She looked startled too and said something like, "I guess so." *What?*

This was quite a head trip. I dissected the possible reasons that Bono would have been moved to yell at me. It was probably just because of irritation with the bubbles, but I thought maybe Bono recognized me by that point, this insistent fan that kept popping up in the heart at every other show, and was a little sick of seeing my face.

Well... This yelling incident further dampened my waning level of enthusiasm. Nonetheless, wanting to be entertained, I stayed and watched as the show went on. I pulled back from the rail a bit and let a slightly shorter girl stand in front of me. "Are you sure?" she asked. Yeah, I was sure.

From this vantage point I viewed the show, feeling removed from the event. We stood right behind Bono and Edge's main position during the acoustic set at the tip of the heart. I was drawn in again by an interaction as it began between Bono and a female fan just across the catwalk from us. I could see her smiling face, as Bono's spotlight spilled down on her. She was beaming up at him as she held out a Ramones shirt and offered it to him. As she held the T shirt up for him, she appeared to be saying, "Take it, take it!" through that bright sweet smile. Bono looked down at her, and then beckoned to her to come on up. Her face lit up, her eyes widened, and her jaw dropped as she allowed herself to be helped over the fence by security and boosted up on to the catwalk with the T shirt still in hand. She popped up to her feet and grinned at Bono. He motioned to her to put the Ramones t-shirt on, which she did, over her other shirt. He put his arm around her and presented her to the audience, as he spoke of the Ramones early influence on U2 and the recent death of Joey Ramone.

"In a Little While," the last song that Joey Ramone had reportedly heard before his recent death, jangled through the arena. Bono sang the song with the Ramones girl from the crowd in his arms. He offered her the microphone towards the song's end. She was up to the challenge and sang the last lyric lightly. As the song ended, the Ramones girl left the stage to thunderous applause.

I watched as security placed her back in her spot with her friends by the rail. She looked at her friend to her left and collapsed into an embrace, laughing as tears streamed down her face. Her joy was visible and touching. It warmed my heart but couldn't completely break through my bitterness.

When the first encore rolled around, I realized that I really didn't belong there, not in that state of mind, and I left the heart as Bono sang an old B-side favorite of mine, U2's version of Nat King Cole's "Night and Day." As I exited the arena, I paused and listened as the he said to the crowd, "If this is your first U2 show ever, then I hope...well, I hope it's the best night of your life." Taken inversely, this seemed like a final and appropriate way of indirectly telling me, and my multiple concert-going friends, to fuck off.

In the end, the event that resulted in all this distraction and psychodrama was probably just a simple misunderstanding. U2 was under a lot of pressure on June 6th, and likely had a lot on their minds with the taping, the live country-wide broadcast, and the pressures from the video production and NBC to make the show perfect. Amidst the chaos, perhaps the tacit understanding that had developed throughout the tour regarding the GA line slipped the minds of our very human heroes, if they had ever been aware of it in the first place. This perceived lack of consideration had ugly consequences that were felt by U2, though they may or may not have known what was going on during the show time on June 6th.

I relate this experience only because it was important to us, at the time. I share this experience because it served as a further agent for me to be ready to let go of the band, and the tour, and the inherent problems that we confront when we seek ultimate beauty and love outside ourselves. As I drove back from Philly on June 11th, 2001, in a dark pouring rain, I felt proud of myself for having literally turned my back on U2. I focused on moving forward and finding new inspiration in my life. I contemplated the idea of taking all the good that I had experienced over the past three months and turning it into a basis of hope for the future. I had learned to look for strength within, and that if one reaches too hard to touch the ideal (that Buddhist concept of grasping, again), one will often find disappointment in the end. It seemed the best place to seek beauty from now on would be within and all around, in the seemingly mundane. Though I had felt hurt and bitter for the past five days, I experienced a profound sense of peace and tranquility as I drove those long miles back to Fairfax VA.

When I got home at 2:00 AM, I wrote in my journal:

This kid is about ready to scrub off the U2 mobile and get back to work... I feel I reached some sense of closure tonight—I will ask Ro how he feels about foregoing Thursday's show and getting some of our "hard earned cash" back. How ironic is this? I drove over 4000 miles to get to U2 shows this spring but may not be bothered to go to the local shows.

It still hurt a little, but I was ready to walk away...and come home to myself.

The next day, I called Ro and suggested my thoughts on foregoing the shows coming up on the 14th and 15th at the MCI center in DC. Ro did want to go to Thursday's show, and in my heart I was glad. I hoped to end my spring tour with a good night, and Thursday would probably be a nice way to do it. We would go on Thursday, and I committed to selling my solo ticket for Friday's show. Two of my sisters and their husbands were also going to the show, and we would meet up for a few pre-show drinks downtown. My ambivalence about the whole thing reappeared on Wednesday, the day before what would be my final show, and I wrote in my journal:

I'm sad about it, really, it's hard to know they'll be in town on Friday, and I won't go, but it's the right thing for me. We have new dreams to chase today... we have a whole world to explore. The Elevation Tour was the perfect vehicle to help us realize that freedom.

The day of the first D.C. show arrived, and arrangements were made with Ro and my sisters to meet downtown for drinks before the show. Ro picked me up at the townhouse where I was renting a room for the mid-afternoon drive into the city. I brought with me my U2OPIA license plate for a wave goodbye to the band and my single ticket for tomorrow's show to sell to someone who would probably enjoy it more than me. I also brought with me my collection of GA wristbands and heart wrist bands from the twelve shows I had attended earlier in the spring. I knew by now that some of the fans were forgoing the hours long GA line waiting game and using old wristbands to get into the heart, even if they didn't have GA tickets. Ro and I had Golden Circle seats for this final show, but of course my heart was on the floor inside *that* heart, with my fellow U2 heads, and at the time, I didn't really see the harm in using my collection to get us down there for this last show.

We parked close to the MCI center, in a paid parking lot behind the arena. We got out of the car and saw a group of about a dozen fans waiting around near what looked like an entrance to the arena's garage, waiting for the band to possibly show up. We strolled past them with only a fleeting interest and found the GA line, where I wanted to search for friends from other shows and unload my ticket for tomorrow.

I saw no one in the GA line that I recognized, but the scene was the same. I sold my ticket at cost to the first interested buyer and met a girl who called me out by name, because she recognized my license plate from early spring posts on U2 message boards.

Ro and I wandered around near the arena a bit as we searched for the Capital City Brewery where we would meet my sisters and their husbands. We walked past bars with preshow parties that offered specials on Guinness and featured U2 music blasting out the front doors. The traveling show had arrived. We met the family after getting a little lost and imbibed a little preshow cheer ourselves. I was touched with a slight melancholy as

I had my family sign my fan book. These would be the last answers to that question: *what makes YOU elevate?* to be added to my collection.

It was June 14th, 2001, and my brother-in-law was working for the CIA at the time. I noticed his inscription, which were the last words written in the book:

MY ELEVATION?

KNOWING THAT BAD GUYS WANT TO DO BAD THINGS,

AND THE GOOD GUYS DO GOOD THINGS

TO FOIL THE BAD GUYS!

ONE OF THE GOOD GUYS.

After a few photos for my tour scrapbook, Ro and I parted ways with the siblings and went to find our seats so that we could enjoy PJ Harvey's set one more time.

I couldn't focus on PJ's set once we were in the MCI center, because I was trying to figure out what color the wristbands were on the floor and see if we had the combination of solid color and checked color to join the crowd in the heart. I rummaged through my collection and was pleased to find that I did indeed have one purple solid and one green checked that would gain the wearer admittance to the heart. I tied my U2OPIA license plate around my neck and ventured out to the arena's halls to find a bathroom so that I could try to tape my old wristbands on and get down there.

Once out of the open arena and into the hallways, I ran into Mike. I found him walking around, looking for another friend, and we greeted each other warmly. He gave me the lowdown on the details of the wristband placement and lent me an extra set for Ro. I ran back to Ro, who wanted to stay in our reserved seats for a while, so with the plan to meet up in the heart later, I gave him his wristbands and took off.

It was ridiculously easy to get down to the inner sanctum. I lifted my wrist up high for security to see as I approached, and they let me pass without even checking my ticket. I suppose they underestimated the drive, focus, and dedicated/obsessive quality of hardcore U2 fans like myself. The idea that people might be hoarding wristband collections to use from show to show obviously hadn't crossed their minds yet. Or perhaps it had, and they figured, hey if the fans are going to try that hard, let them go on into the heart. I don't know. All I know was that it felt good to be waved down into that darkened floor again as PJ finished her set, and I walked proudly with my U2 license plate held high over my head, like a flag.

Following my arrival into the heart, PJ's set ended, and I looked around the arena for my family who had told me what section they were in. I called my sister up in section 238 on my cell and hopped up and down waving the plate as I gloated about my new location (talk about ego!). The show started in typical fashion and passed with a slight modification to the predictable set list. Ro joined me on the floor during "Desire" and we enjoyed a live rendition of the non-album single called "The Ground Beneath Her Feet" which poignantly echoed through the arena in place of "Stay."

U2, or at least Bono, seemed happy to be in DC tonight, and thanked this crowd for their continuing support as he recalled the first U2 show here back in 1980 at a bar called the Bayou in Georgetown. It cost about $3 to get in and there were less than one hundred in attendance. I couldn't make it to that one because I was three at the time.

The live rendition of "Bullet the Blue Sky" seemed especially charged this evening. After all, the song was written as an angry rant against American foreign policy in the eighties. The song has served since then as a sort of sounding off platform for whatever worldly political happening is angering Bono at the time of any given tour.

During this tour, it was made into a rather oblique statement about gun violence in America. Watching the present incarnation of "Bullet the Blue Sky" in the very city where DC politicos voted on laws that determine the level of gun control in our nation made for a slightly charged atmosphere.

Bono's spoken word piece during the song had developed throughout the live shows to this point in the tour into a raging rap that condemned the business of marketing firearms in America at the cost of escalating violence. Bono affected a look in the eyes of the American voters all over the arena by swinging his spotlight into every corner of the hall as he chanted, in an edgy mix of anger and broken heartedness, about the hundreds of thousands of people that would be killed by a bullet in this country over the course of the next twenty years.

This part of the show continued to fascinate me because Bono's rap evolved from show to show, and I continued to pick up more of the meaning in his words.

During "Walk On," I asked Ro to hold my license plate over his head, because we were tucked in at the back of the heart and his height only might be able to bring the plate into the bandmembers line of vision. He obliged me. As the closer ran its course, there were more tears for me, and a sudden sense of panic about missing tomorrow's show. I shouted at Ro, "Will you come down here with me tomorrow and let's try to get tickets one more time?" He shook his head and said no, gently, "Let's leave it at this Marcy." I knew he was right. Enough was enough.

I felt sad and deflated as the show ended. I hugged Mike goodbye weepily. It was all over. Underneath these reactive emotions, I was aware of my readiness to leave the Elevation Tour behind and get back to a more normal, mundane lifestyle for a while. After all, Ro and I had new dreams to chase now. We were planning to move away from the overpopulated suburbs of Washington, DC, to Denver, CO, by the start of 2002. We had a new adventure to plan for.

I was glad to go to sleep that night in my own bed in Fairfax.

For the first few weeks after our tour ended, I was mostly content. I went on about my business with a renewed zest for life and a sort of free-floating enthusiasm. Ro was living outside Annapolis, a good hour's drive from Fairfax, and I was reinvigorated on weekends by trips with him to his father's large house in the more rural surroundings than suburban Virginia provided to its residents. Ro and I went to an Aerosmith concert in Virginia near the end of June, and it was interesting to see a different band's live show after so many from U2.

I kept myself occupied with securing a promotion at work, and this change kept me happy with some new challenges as I enjoyed feeling settled again. I also took a short break from being a U2 fan and didn't even think about U2 or the whole adventure for a few weeks.

At the beginning of July, Ro and I went to visit a friend of mine in Harrisonburg Virginia, the town of my alma mater in the Shenandoah Valley. It was good to get away from the hustle and bustle of the metro area, and as I visited with Suzy, I ended up talking and reflecting for the first time in several weeks on my travels during the spring. I showed her my scrapbook and continued to feel okay about the experience having passed already.

I woke early in the morning one day that weekend in Harrisonburg and I went to sit alone on Suzy's small screened in porch with a cup of coffee and a cigarette (Ro and I had tried to quit again and failed after our tour's end). I was surrounded by deciduous greenery, and the morning sun was gentle on my face with cool breezes playing in my hair. After searching through Suzy's house for a scrap piece of paper and a pencil, I sat and reflected on paper:

I wrote pages and pages as I moved into my 2001. The time has come to write of moving on.

This chasing of a dream has brought me home to a reality that welcomes me warmly. I had to step out of my life to be able to step back into it with gratitude. I feel, if I was free to do this, the world is wide open. I've come home to dreams and inspiration and a seemingly endless vista towards the future. The shows I was ready to leave behind, but the realizations that come with this are infinitely rewarding and as wondrous as anything I saw out there. This understanding could last a lifetime. I've come home to all that I can't leave behind and I have added some gems to the treasure of my being.

Small pangs of grief remain, having written all of that. The grief is a soul's challenge to recreate that utopia within every day. Keep an open mind. Seek and find beauty. Understand peace. And get lost in your music.

Always,

Your Self

I was ready to move on to new adventures, but no adventures came to me for a little while. By the end of July, I found myself grappling with a low-level sort of deflation. After all the excitement during the spring, things in the working world seemed rather flat, even as I took on new challenges in my professional promotion. I missed the frequent opportunities to express my spirit at U2 concerts and I missed my friends in the community, who were now out of reach, having either retreated to their corners of the world and back to normal life like me, or having followed U2 to Europe for the summer. I enjoyed spending time with friends and family, but I missed being able to go to my own personal sort of church with others that I knew automatically understood how I felt. It was a sort of pointless nostalgia, though, because I knew there was no way I could have gone back. It seemed that I had taken the whole fanaticism thing to its end, to the point where I was no longer feeling like a fanatic. To the point where I had to step back from it.

These feelings of being U2 saturated were sort of confusing. Sure, I had gotten to the point of being sick of the band before, but never to this extent. It was unsettling: I missed the shows. But I didn't want to go to anymore shows. I had to look elsewhere for inspiration. And I did that by looking to the future and trying to stay mindful of the lessons about connection and beauty that I had learned through the fanatic experience.

ELEVATION AND BEYOND

I recently went to a yogi ashram in El Dorado, Colorado, and sat in on a question-and-answer session with a swami, during which the swami discussed the love that one feels for a guru, or spiritual teacher. Swami said that an adored guru can only take the student so far in discovering the truth, and that oftentimes when a student lets go of the adoration and adulation of a guru it is because the student starts to understand that the individual guru is but a channel of the light that emits from everything. Having learned this, the student can stop seeking the light solely from that guru. Then the student begins to look deeper, beyond the beloved guru, to the source of the light, and that adoration and worship moves from the focus on an individual to a sweeping love for every source of that light of wisdom. These words struck me, and I was caught off guard by the emotion that they stirred within me. It described the process that I had attempted to complete in the summer of 2001. U2, and especially Bono, had served as a sort of imagined guru to me since I was a kid. Finally, it was looking like I was ready to grasp the idea that the light I saw in them emanates from and through all of creation, including me.

It was a hell of a challenge, though. And I didn't know how to do it. My sense of deflation was sort of the overwhelming vibe of the summer. Ro and I were ready to move away from the area in search of wider open spaces in Denver, and we would have gone right away, but we were broke. We sat out the summer and worked and waited for the day that we could move on.

Rumored tour dates for the third leg of the Elevation Tour in the states scheduled for the fall started to circulate online. I met them with ambivalence. Part of me wanted to jump in the car and do it all over again, chase them around for a few more weeks, but I had already accepted the reality that there was a limit to the magic of U2, even for me. I decided that I would be satisfied with only seeing them twice on their triumphant return in the fall, and then it would be goodbye to my rock and roll gurus for a while. I only willed to hold on to the spirit that that I had found on the road with them.

Soon enough, I would be shocked out of my rather lazy ennui on what started off as just another beautiful early fall morning.

On the night of September 10th, Ro and I went down to the 9:30 club in DC to see PJ Harvey on her headline tour. Her CD, "Stories from the City, Stories from the Sea" was now in regular rotation on my CD player.

That great show rocked into the wee hours of the morning and I took a set list from the stage home with me. We didn't get back to my place to crash out until about 2:00 AM. This gave me only a few hours to rest before I would have to wake up to be at work at 8:00 a.m. at the Adult Care Residence where I was employed as a Clinical Case Manager and was scheduled to serve the next day as shift supervisor. As September 11th dawned, I dragged my weary, hungover self out of bed and out of the townhouse into a clear and breezy sunlit morning. Ah. Another beautiful day.

An hour later, after a few cups of coffee, I was passing out medications to our residents (thirty-six dear and varyingly crazy souls). I was struggling with medications and the impatient residents lined up at the med window when our Activities Coordinator, Diane, came breezing past, all energy and bright colors. She said furtively to me (so as not to upset the residents), "Did you hear? The World Trade Center has been hit by an airplane!" Huh? I had no idea what she was talking about, and I dismissed the nonsensical statement for a moment as I worked to finish the immediately pressing issue of getting all thirty-six of our residents their morning meds with lots of help from the shift team.

After closing the Med closet a few minutes later, I hurried into the staff conference room where a handful of my colleagues (all of whom I loved) were standing around staring at the yapping TV set, which was hardly ever turned on, and never turned on during the busy morning hours at the ACR, with wide eyes.

On the screen was a shot of a flaming, smoking skyscraper.

"What's going on?" I demanded as I grabbed some coffee.

"There was an accident," said my supervisor Randy, his eyes still glued to the set, "a plane hit the World Trade Center in New York."

I went back into the office area. Breaking news is good and all, but we had work to do. Our monthly full staff meeting was scheduled to start in less than thirty minutes. My tired, frazzled brain didn't want to focus on anything other than getting through this workday and back to my soft bed for more sleep, not even strange accidents occurring in New York City (a place which I had only visited twice briefly, and which I had found overwhelming). I started dialing the phone for a quick call to the sister of one of my clients, but then—

"Oh my God!" Diane yelled out from the conference room.

I hurried back in to see what was going on, more curious than worried. On the TV screen a second tower was on fire. Then, I was shocked to see footage of a commercial airline veering directly, and obviously on purpose, into the second tower.

What the hell?!?

Though I had no concept of this at the time, perhaps millions of Americans across the nation were having the same what-the-hell moment as the hideous truth (this is no accident) hit us in a wave, and we all stared at our TV screens in shock. The flustered newscaster was obviously dealing with the shock too, because he couldn't quite seem to get what was going on, but then he appeared to be sitting in a studio somewhere getting reports in his earpiece. Not watching the event with his own two eyes.

It was hard enough to wrap your mind around what was happening even if you did see it as it occurred. Seeing is believing? Not on 9/11/01.

Not for me anyway. As we stared, with wide eyes and open mouths, more and more of the ACR's thirty-plus staff were arriving. They trickled in, silent and staring, one by one, to the conference room and office area for the staff meeting which was scheduled to commence now, if not sooner.

Our fearless leader and director of the ACR, Sherry, appeared and began herding us into the large meeting room. The TV was shut off and we all went in for the meeting.

All through that meeting, my mind was replaying those planes striking and trying to understand what I had witnessed. Sherry struggled on through the agenda, saying kindly, "I know that we're all distracted by what's going on out there, but we have to get through this". As a team dedicated to our professional mission, we tried, and we managed to go through the motions of that meeting for a full hour. Things sort of fell apart when the dining manager re-entered the room after a short absence and told us quietly during a pause: "The South Tower fell."

Again, this made no sense to me. What the hell?

I guess it made more sense to everyone else in the room, because the meeting quickly deteriorated after we heard that news. We struggled respectfully through the agenda for as long as we could. Sherry adjourned us after wrapping up as quickly as possible. Everyone started to move towards the TV set. I stayed back and helped put chairs away. I guess I was stalling. Scared.

But then, a scream from the cafeteria, and the cook went running through the dining room. I left the meeting room and headed back to the office. What the hell is going on? I demanded again.

In reality, I probably said something quietly to a colleague, something like, "Is Patty (the screaming cook) OK?" But I really wanted to shout out that first question. My colleague told me that Patty had a sister working in the Pentagon. So? I thought to myself.

But then I saw the shot on TV of the Pentagon. Hit. Then footage of the tower falling in New York. Shit.

After that, the hours passed in a blur of, first, shock, and then fear that felt more like panic. In my short twenty-four years, I had never seen anything like this. I had never seen anything remotely close to this, not even in the history books, happening on US soil. Maybe Pearl Harbor? But that was during the war!

It didn't make sense, and I had no idea what was going on. I went outside for a cigarette. As I smoked, PJ Harvey's song "Kamikaze", which I had seen her perform live less than ten hours ago, ran in an endless loop through my sleep-deprived brain.

My friend Debbie, the House Manager, joined me momentarily. Debbie was in her late forties, and I had come to consider her true friend after working by her side for the past two years. She looked at me through careworn eyes as she let her Virginia Slim. I asked her what she thought of all this (a more polite version of "what the hell's going on?"). She simply said, "This is war." We spoke animatedly about what we had seen, what it meant, and what it could mean for her. She had a bright, wonderful twenty-year-old son whom she had already called at home to tell him not to enlist! She also had plans for a long-awaited trip to Alaska for which she was meant to depart within days. Now the safety of that was in question.

We went back inside after this much needed chance to process the events of the past several hours. We were met with more horror: footage of people jumping out of windows of the burning buildings to fall from the skyscrapers to their deaths, people screaming and running from a demon dust cloud, people limping away, covered in a thick dusty powder. The TV spoke of a driven but doomed rescue effort, and my thoughts were with those countless souls that I imagined were trapped in rubble. Were they alive? I heard something about cell phone calls coming from under there. Can we save them?

We turned off the TV, remembering that there were still thirty-six folks here who needed our attention. Moments slipped by in a blur. I called Ro once the phones were working again. He was managing a gas station literally next door to the National Security Agency, and he described a scene up there in Fort Meade, Maryland. Roads closed, cops everywhere, people evacuating the NSA building. Here was a personal worry. I urged Ro to go home, be safe.

The TV came back on during lunch. The nurse practitioner at the ACR mentioned that her husband was a firefighter and had been called to the Pentagon, where pandemonium had also broken loose, though on a smaller scale. I went back outside after choking down a few bites in front of the grim coverage. I had to get out of there, just for a moment, to see the blue sky, make sure it was still there. I hopped in my car to go grab another pack of smokes. As I drove to the gas station, the radio was on and reporting happenings in Arlington: closure of the DC Beltway, the president's movements, and some initial reaction. I gripped the wheel, feeling panic, and the birth of anger as I heard the words "al Qaeda" for the first time. Anger bordering on rage, especially when I heard that people were dancing in the streets of Afghanistan and other parts of the Middle East. But still panic... I felt a palpable sense of the bubble having burst. A security that I had taken for granted throughout my entire life was gone, just like that. Life seemed fragile and threatened. The illusion of America's isolation and relative safety had vanished with the twin towers.

The rest of the day passed in a daze of relentlessly fatigue, shock, and anxiety. Finally, the shift's end rolled around, and I drove home. I flipped on the TV in my room at the townhouse and saw local reports headed by the words "America Under Attack". Quickly, I dozed off to feverish dreams of violence.

When I woke, several hours later, the TV was still running a montage of horrible images and information from the day. It was a slap in the face as reality came rushing back. Fox News was reporting on hundreds of firefighters who had marched up the stairs of the doomed South tower of the World Trade Center, just doing their jobs, just going to save some lives. Then the tower collapsed on them.

That did it. The emotion, the tragedy, the pain and suffering and outright horror of the day, hit me, and I wept. But there was no sense of relief—just helpless tears for those doomed heroes in the face of so much death.

My mother called me later that night. The family was spending the week at a beach house near Roanoke. I had only been able to join them for a long weekend, having used up all my vacation time and then some earlier in the year on my U2 tour. My mother wanted to check in on me. We didn't talk long. The hot issue at the beach house was that of how my brothers and their families would get back to their far-flung homes in Colorado and South Dakota. No planes were flying.

I went outside and wondered if planes should ever fly again. I wondered a lot of things that night.

The next two days passed painfully. I was scheduled to work twenty hours at the ACR before a long weekend. I tried to bury myself in work, escape the reality of the seriously fucked up outside world, but there was no escaping the hurt and distress that ran in long lines across the faces of my colleagues, and my own face in the mirror. Everyone was down. People could barely speak. We looked out across the distance between ourselves with haunted eyes, through the mist of bloody tragedy that had slammed in as an alien backdrop to our existence. We heard on the news of the rescue efforts, and their seeming futility. There was nothing to find. Just dust, where thousands of Americans had once stood. Americans who were good people, just like us, but had been condemned to this horrible death just for being Americans. It was for these victims of hatred that I wore a small beaded American flag pin through those first days after the attack. I was haunted by Stephen King-esque thoughts of what these imagined survivors were going through, right now, up north in the rubble of the twin towers. My vivid imagination made waking moments nightmarish during those first days. I could see them, these imagined victims, lying in dark holes that rescuers wouldn't find until it was too late.

And still that PJ song "Kamikaze" ran through my brain with great frequency. The song's lyrics hit home with me as they played through my Hyundai's speakers, reflecting the desperate fear and horror that I was feeling the week of September 11th.

PJ's album "Stories from the City, Stories from the Sea" stayed in my CD player on a permanent basis from 9/11 on through the following weeks. So many of the songs on that CD were eerily appropriate to this horrible situation. The first song on the CD, "Big Exit," speaks of a frightening and insecure world that matched my own. A place where the subject bemoans the world's insanity and finds safety in her own stash of firearms.

Before 9/11, I couldn't really identify with that survival instinct that can make humans take up arms for protection. My life had been too easy, characterized by a sense of safety that was taken for granted. While I was, in fact, safe from imminent harm, I knew that anything could happen now. Lying in my bed at the room in Fairfax, I heard planes flying overhead and knew that they were military (no commercial planes would fly for another few days). This was strange enough, that we now had military tangibly watching over us for our safety, but stranger still was a sense of fear I would feel in just hearing a low flying plane. "Big Exit" ended with a reflection on being unable to find a place to stand in safety. That could have been the theme of those first days after 9-11. I didn't even feel safe in my house in quiet suburban Fairfax VA. The idea of moving out west to Denver immediately became even more appealing.

Once it occurred to me, I felt that all the wonders and drama of U2's Elevation Tour meant nothing and weren't even worth thinking about now. It seemed laughable, in fact, that I had been so caught up in that microcosm for the entirety of 2001 up to this point. While I had been playing, living, and learning, it seemed that strangers were plotting for the demise of as many Americans as possible. It could have been me. It could have been any of us. For all I knew then, and for all I know now, some of my new friends from the tour could have perished in the rubble that day.

I didn't really comprehend all of this then. All I knew was that what had been so important before no longer mattered in those first weeks following the horror of 9/11, and that just added to my sense of having had reality (or the illusion of reality) pulled out from under me.

I watched the Concert for New York, a televised special that happened nine days after the disaster, weeping as Fred Durst sang "Imagine." The ideals of this song seemed so lost. I missed U2's performance that night, broadcast live from London, but didn't care.

I occasionally wondered what U2 would say about all of this, and even wished to hear some words of comfort and inspiration from Bono, but nothing came immediately, when I needed comfort the most (when we all did). The only comfort I found in those first few weeks was a sort of pathetic feeling of warmth and admiration for President George W. Bush, our fearless leader, who served as a beacon of light and hope for the resilience of the American ideals of Freedom and Justice. I watched on television as he stood in front of Congress on September 20 and courageously spoke of making things right again, of finding those that did this to us and making them answer for it. Bush spoke of the strength and goodness of the American people. This black-and-white thinking was comforting. He gave me hope that the world would make sense again someday soon. Talk of justice meant that someone would have to answer for this crime against humanity. That name "Osama bin Laden" became the focus of this lust for retribution, and a focus for new and bitter hatred bred in the hearts of Americans. Even mine. The birth of new hatred was overshadowed in my heart by a newfound sense of patriotism, faith in the American vision, and brotherhood with my fellow countrymen. We were in this together, and we were strong in numbers and in heart.

I was able to stop and reflect in my notebook on September 21st. After the shock subsided, these were the first words that I penned:

Ten days ago, the greatest atrocity my country has seen in... ever... was perpetrated against us. Tonight, I cry with millions of Americans mourning the loss of thousands. We stand now on the brink of more violence and more loss of life. And my generation perhaps struggles with our naivete. The bubble has burst, and it falls about us in tears of shock and loss.

We're strong, and now we're stronger than ever. I did not imagine I would live in a wartime so soon, and while we still don't know what form this war will take, we recognize that it is a war. The thousands dead in New York's rubble are proof of that.

Revenge?

Retaliation?

Payback?

I believed I am a pacifist—now I'm not so sure.

Tonight, I pray and wish upon the thousands that died last Tuesday... and I pray for peace and healing to come to their loved ones. Let us support each other through this grisly nightmare. Let us learn now from an act of hatred how much we love each other, and what love really is.

It took ten days, but I could see some light of hope emerging from under this heavy cloud of tragedy. I wanted to follow it.

CHAPTER 5:
INTEGRATION

It was the desire to turn toward hope in a time of loss that led me to order tickets for two more Elevation shows on the third leg of the tour, for U2's triumphant return to the US in the fall of 2001. Immediately after 9/11, it seemed that all artists and major entertainment events around the country were being postponed or rescheduled. I waited for some news that the band had decided not to come to America in this crazy time. That news never came...of course U2 would come. They had played Sarajevo in '97, for God's sake. I ordered two tickets from Propaganda for the show in Baltimore on October 19th. I called Denver Ticketmaster and ordered three more for the show two days before my twenty-fifth birthday on November 9th. Ro and I would visit Colorado in November for a long weekend. We would stay with Alie, a friend of mine from college, who had moved to Denver the preceding year. It seemed like it would be a good way to spend my birthday. I'd be saying goodbye to the band and saying hello to a future in Colorado. Forget the past, kiss the future. Or something like that.

After 9/11, time marched on, speedy and grim, and only ten days prior to the scheduled Elevation show in Baltimore, my ticket still hadn't arrived. Instead, I received a letter in the mail saying that there was a problem with my order and instructing me to call a ticket agency in Maryland for further assistance. When I called, I was informed that the demand for GA tickets had outweighed the supply, but that I could get $135 Golden Circle seats. Of course, I would have to pay them the extra $100 plus for the expensive reserved seats that I hadn't wanted anyway. This was too much. I was annoyed and sorely disappointed. I said sorry, I can't afford that, then secured my refund for the GA tickets that wouldn't come and hung up.

Karma had shown her pretty face. I had gotten all those tickets in the spring by being greedy and manipulative with the Propaganda fan ticketing system. Other people who followed the rules then probably got screwed several times over because of this sort of selfishness. With respect to the idea that what goes around comes around, I accepted this shortfall of tickets without any bitterness. But my anxiety increased as the days went by, and I found myself no closer to tickets. After a short three-and-a-half-month break, I was again driven to see U2, especially after what had happened here in America in the meantime. Their music was still a great comfort to me.

I saw U2 on David Letterman in October. They performed "New York" and "Stuck in a Moment." Bono had changed the lyrics to "New York" to reflect what happened there last month. Tonight, he sang, "In New York you can forget just how strong is this city's will!"

Though I cringed at Bono's posing as the Statue of Liberty—smirking, with microphone as torch and four fingers splayed behind his head in a crown—the performance enlivened me and psyched me up for a couple more U2 shows. "Stuck in a Moment" had become the perfect lullaby for

America. We *were* stuck. We all walked around with long, lined faces for weeks after 9/11. It seemed that 9/11 had aged Americans, on average, by about ten years. That night, hearing Bono sing sweetly that this time would pass, I found myself soothed to no end.

The days preceding the Baltimore show were spent checking prices online at ticket broker sites. I had the same problem here, too damn expensive. I couldn't pay that much extra for U2 now because Ro and I were trying to save up for the cross-country move by the first of the new year.

I remembered then that it had been discussed on many occasions through the years that the band often releases tickets on the day of show to frustrate the scalpers out there. Ro and I discussed the scenario, and he agreed to take me down to the Baltimore arena in the morning on day of show so that I could try to score concert day box-office seats.

I figured if I was going to be down there, I would have to get into the show, so I took a little extra money with me from my savings just in case I would have to succumb to a scalper. But I limited the funding as much as I could. I still wasn't going to lose $270 on this. I took $200. I also figured, if I'm going to spend the whole day there and pursue decently priced tickets, might as well get a good spot in the queue and try to get super close one more time. I had ordered reserved seats for the Denver show. I wouldn't be very close to the boys there. Baltimore would be the last chance if I could score tickets.

At my request, Ro drove me in to the Baltimore Arena and dropped me off in the dark cold morning before 5:00 AM on October 19th. He wouldn't be able to hang out in line today because he was off to work. I was very surprised to see a long line wrapping around the building at this ungodly hour. I wandered to the end of the line and received number 110 marked on my wrist and got Ro number 111. I set up camp. I was tired and more than a little nervous about my lack of tickets. Was one allowed to set up camp in line if one didn't have tickets? I didn't know. I kept a low profile at first while I observed the scene. The folks in front of me were bundled up in sleeping bags and blankets, huddled together on the cold hard concrete. I stayed put in my blue camping chair, wrapped in a blanket, and watched the sunrise through sleepy eyes. I sat with the hundred-plus crowd and watched the city of Baltimore rise from slumber as I had watched Boston three months ago. We watched the passersby stare at the lot of us. Such a strange bunch, those U2 fans.

Around 8:00 AM I asked the small group behind me in line to save my spot so that I could take a lap around the building and scope out the scene. As I turned the corner around the arena, I saw tents at the very front of the line. They were zipped closed and there was no movement from inside them. Instead, a sign was taped on the railing that was in front of them, securing the very first portion of the GA line. The sign read:

"Answers to FAQ's:

1. We're waiting here to get into the U2 concert tonight.
2. We already have tickets, but it's GENERAL ADMISSION.
3. We've been here since 12 noon yesterday.
4. Yes, we are crazy.
5. No, you don't get it. "

It made me laugh. I understood where they were coming from only too well!

The morning brightened after that. It was a literal and emotional brightening, as the sun rose with my spirits. I walked around the next corner of the building and saw the Box Office. There was a fan hanging out by the door. I joined him and we discussed the likelihood of procuring GA seats in this way. Chances didn't seem good. Reportedly, the day of show tickets that had been released over the last week had been mostly the expensive Golden Circle seats. The Box Office wasn't scheduled to open for another hour. I ran off to check on my spot in the GA line. It was cool, the college kids next to me promised to save my spot and said I should go wait at the box office if I needed tickets. I thanked them profusely and went back.

I returned to the Box Office and sat in line with a small handful of fans that had gathered. Chatting easily with the guy sitting next to me, I learned that U2 had been playing "Out of Control" and "11 O'clock Tick Tock" at the shows over the past nine days since their return to touring America. This added to the excitement. I hadn't thought that I would ever get the chance to see them playing songs that were this obscure, relatively speaking. After all, they had more than enough recent hits to fill up a concert. As we waited, we started checking out the tour buses at the backstage parking area, which was visible from where we sat. Bits of activity were occurring already at this early hour. Out of nowhere, Dallas, Edge's roadie, emerged on the scene. He walked past us on the sidewalk toward the backstage entrance. Someone called out, "Hello Dallas!" He turned and nodded at us, then reached into his pocket. "Here you go!" he said, tossing us some of Edge's guitar picks as he hurried by. I got one and examined it. There appeared to be an Edge signature on the back and there were a few of the Elevation Tour logos on the front. Cool! I pocketed the thing.

As the morning went on, I heard rumors that there were fans back in the GA line selling GA seats for reasonable amounts. I ran off, back to the growing queue, and sniffed around. Someone pointed me in the right direction and thirty minutes later I was the very relieved bearer of two GA seats for the price of $200. I had bought each individually from two different fans, not professional scalpers, so it wasn't as bad as it might have been.

With tickets in hand, I returned to my original spot in line to wait out the day. I sighed into my comfortable camp. It was good to be home, and I began chatting with the now arisen pair to my right. Here was a mother, Lori, who looked about the band's age, attending the show with her son. Lori and I talked about how hot Bono was as her son sat laughing at us. Eventually the conversation turned to 9/11. She told me how glad she was that she had taken her son to see New York before the Twin Towers disappeared. The threat of further terrorism was on our minds. Wouldn't a rock concert be a convenient place for another attack, we mused. After the recent string of anthrax scares, biological warfare was on our minds. We reassured each other with talk of increased security. How strange it felt to be still under threat, even in this idealized setting. I pushed these thoughts away. It was already early afternoon, and I asked my linemates to hold my spot again for a little while. I was off to the parking area in the back to check out the scene. A handful of folks stood around there. I recognized a guy that I had seen at numerous shows in the spring and went to meet him. I was surprised to find myself talking to Otto Kitsinger, by far the best fan photographer of U2 that I had ever come across. He showed me some of his photos that he carried with him in a portfolio. I was entranced by one of Bono from the back and standing at the heart's tip, taken from inside the heart. Bono's arms were raised over his head, greeting the brightly lit masses in front of him. I figured it had to have been taken during the beginning of "Streets," at that penultimate moment when the lights shine on the whole audience. I asked Otto if I could get a copy of this print and we exchanged information.

For the rest of the afternoon, I hopped back and forth between the GA line and the back arena parking lot. As the day wore on, more fans gathered at the fence in the back. Finally, at about 3:00 PM, Ro made it back into the city and joined me at the arena.

We met at my spot in the GA line, and we left shortly thereafter to grab a couple beers. As we sat in a nearby pub, I was very aware of the impending arrival of U2 at the arena, and since it seemed that the fans had found the entrance that the band would surely come through to get into the arena, I wanted to get back from the bar to welcome them with the small crowd.

Throughout the day I had been revisiting thoughts of the spring tour, and how it had ended for me in June. I thought about the bitterness and bad vibes that had been generated in Boston. I remembered how very upset I had been about the whole thing, how betrayed I had felt. What had mattered so much then didn't seem at all relevant now. In fact, it seemed rather childish. I felt myself letting go of what had been such a big deal. Letting go of the childish hurt. I felt myself opening to love again. I had been very depressed since the day of September 11th. Life had buzzed by in a painful fog. Only here, at a post 9/11 U2 show, did I feel the coldness inside beginning to be penetrated by the warmth of love.

At about 4:00 PM, Ro and I joined the growing crowd standing behind the fence watching the tour buses move about. We moved into a group of about fifty people lining the chest-high metal fence. The throng stood clumped together in the middle and thinned at the edges in a bell curve formation. There was a nervous, excited buzz about the group. We strained to see past tour buses, and we shouted out to road crew members who wandered by indifferently, "Will they be out? Are they here yet?" Fans clutched vinyl album covers waiting to be autographed, an Irish flag, flowers to give to our heroes, and cameras poised to shoot. We the fans stood together in an excited fervor, and waited anxiously atop the concrete, just outside the Baltimore arena. We were enveloped in the warm October evening sun, and we jostled each other companionably as the moment ticked by.

Then, a cheer began at the far-left side and someone behind me hopped into the branches of a small tree jutting out of a pot of dirt, which punctuated the sidewalk behind us. I strained up onto my tiptoes and Ro called out in the middle of the crowd, "Come over here, Marcy!" Several black Lincoln Continentals drove past in front of us into the underground garage and the crowd's cheer grew in volume. We couldn't see them, but we all knew it. U2 was in those cars.

A beefy man wearing all black approached us arrogantly from the other side of the fence, thundering over the cheers, "OK! OKAY people! Quiet down! They're going to come out for a few minutes, but if you freak out, they will leave. So just be calm, be cool, and you'll get your autographs." As this man was finishing his announcement, Edge emerged from the garage, smiling and waving a hand over his head at the crowd, which was relatively hushed after hearing Mr. Beefy's message. We stared at Edge, grinning, controlling ourselves, like nature lovers hoping for an encounter with a skittish deer. The other deer emerged from the garage— Adam, Bono, and Larry too. Excited fans started shouting and shushing each other intermittently.

    The band members reached the fence and began moving down the line, left to right, methodically signing the items shoved towards them. Tense, controlled adoration flowed like a river from the fenced off throng. I waved my U2 license plate over my head. A woman cried out, "Bono, please!" at the other end of the line. Adam passed by, smiling, and signing. Bono was kneeling with his back against the fence just down to our left, getting photographed with a group of fans. Larry neared my spot in the line, and some guy shoved forward into me, pushing, straining to get his item autographed. "Dude chill out or they will leave!" I whispered pointedly at him. Dude gave me his item to pass to Larry, whose face flickered with irritation as I reached over the shoulders of two girls in front of me who were having their items signed and placed the album in his field of vision. "Thank you, Sir," I said meekly as he signed it, then retracted it as he nodded tersely. Turning around, I gave Dude his prize.

    I moved out of the throng to the far end of the line where I could lean against the fence alone instead of risk being pushed into by another sweaty fan. I leaned over and saw the compact form of Bono signing autographs just fifteen feet to my left on the inside of the fence. He was moving down the line towards me, slowly but surely. I stood watching, doubting that he would come this far, but happy just to see him. I was happy to see all of them. Sure enough, they waved goodbye, Bono lingering with the fans the longest, and turned back one by one to head into the arena and prepare for the show. I felt charged with energy and gladness as they turned away, and I hollered my goodbyes with the rest of the crowd, which immediately began to dissipate.

Ro and I returned to the GA line which we found had pushed forward around the side of the arena by a good measure. I was trying to contain my excitement as the post-U2-sighting buzz rushed through my veins. We found our spot amongst those that I had been hanging with all day. They had moved up much closer to the arena entrance by now and were packed together more densely. They kindly made room for Ro and me to get back in line. As many fans that had been at the band's appearance rounded the corner, one guy jumped up in the air and did a little sort of dance on the sidewalk, leaping and shouting out "Yeah!" I laughed. I knew why he was celebrating. He was clutching a vinyl album cover with fresh autographs on it. Starry-eyed fans passed us by, going back to their spots in the GA line. I was rather starry-eyed myself. I called my sister Gini, who was also attending the concert tonight, on her cell phone. I talked to her husband Matt, who reported that he was stuck in a Beltway traffic snafu, and they would hopefully get to Baltimore in time to get to their seats before the show. I gleefully joked with Matt that I had just come from the band's pre-show meet and greet. I talked to Gini, found out what section they would be in, and promised to look for them from inside the heart.

After that phone call, there was another hour or so to kill before we would be allowed inside. We waited and the energy grew outside the arena. We defended our spots in line as people arrived around 6:00 PM just before doors opened and tried to inconspicuously slip into the queue. Very uncool. We did our best to keep them out, but the fence that secured the line went to only about fifty people deep, so it wasn't easy.

The line began to move, and soon enough Ro and I were inside the arena, jogging down to the floor. We went down a ramp and entered from the back of the floor. As we hurried through the entryway, Paul McGuinness ambled by with a companion. "Hi Paul!" I chirped at him, still rushing past. Startled, he turned and nodded and said something like, "Thank you."

I was giddy as we found our spots in the heart. I grabbed a patch of floor behind just one small person who leaned against the rail slightly to the right of center stage. I had no rail to lean on, but the rising excitement and joy of the whole day had left me feeling strong enough to stand unsupported for the next few hours. I looked for Gini and Matt but couldn't find them. I took in the sight of the still relatively empty arena. The Baltimore Arena looked old and small in comparison to other arenas I had seen U2 play in during the spring. It felt about the size of a high school auditorium in relation to places like the United Center in Chicago and the Fleet Center in Boston. A feeling of intimacy was immediately palpable. Apart from the small size of the place I was now closer to Bono's mainstage position than I had been at any other show. Garbage was scheduled to open for U2 that night, but we had learned pre-show that they had been forced to pull out at the last minute today, because one of the band members was ill. Their last-minute stand in was a local Baltimore band called Graham Parker and the Figgs. At 7:30 PM, the lights in the house went down and the local band took the stage. Mr. Parker and his Figgs looked rather startled to be on stage for opening for U2, but they did well for themselves under the circumstances. Their humility reinforced the feeling of intimacy.

Following the impromptu opener's set, the lights came back up and I resumed visually scanning the crowd for Matt and Gini. Ro ran off to get some beers and I waited quietly in the crowd for the show to begin.

U2 came out at 9:30 PM with the house lights still blazing. Bono greeted us as the opening chords of "Elevation" rang out through the arena, telling us: "We wouldn't want to be anywhere else!" just before the song took off with Edge's opening guitar riff and that familiar shout from Bono: "The goal is elevation!" Wouldn't want to be anywhere else? He made it clear that they wouldn't have dreamt of rescheduling, wouldn't be scared off from their fans by anyone. He answered the question I hadn't had the opportunity to ask. Maybe someone else had.

"Elevation" pumped through the arena in its fashion. We were jumping again up front, mirroring Bono's spastic thrusts of energy on stage. At the end of the song, Bono wailed over the band's driving force: "Elevation!

Soul nation! Soul nation! Soul nation!" Tonight, these words were a nod to the spirit of America in these difficult times. Next came "Beautiful Day," at its standard location as second song in the show. It sounded different tonight, and the lyrics resonated with me.

We had survived the flood. We were out again, out to celebrate the colors of life at this concert. The hundreds of us in the heart raised our hands over our heads, raising our arms in salute to all of creation, mimicking Bono's gesture placed after this lyric in the "Beautiful Day" video which he repeated tonight onstage.

The celebration continued with the start of "New Year's Day," placed early in the set. This song, written almost twenty years ago, was strong with hope tonight. It was a hope that I was, and we all were, looking for and needing just one month after hope had been turned on its head and beaten to a pulp by the events and implications of September 11th, 2001.

Bono's voice was strong tonight. The themes of breaking through and becoming unified again touched my heart. Relief flooded through me as it arrived in the area, and re-entered our lives, tonight with these lyrics. They rang out like a prayer, as the audience sang along to Bono's impassioned wail. He was not holding back tonight. He walked around the catwalk and connected with as much of the audience as he could during this song, looking around the arena, waving to the folks far in the back and up above.

The lead vocalist returned to his position just before us on mainstage as "New Year's Day" came to its end. Then, before I knew it, the heavy backbeat of "Out of Control" was thumping through the hall. The inclusion of this song felt like a gift, and I cried out "THANK YOU!" as I realized it was getting started. I found myself gazing up with the girls around me at the underside of Bono's chin as he called out to the audience, "We're from the north side of the city, we're called U2. This is our first single. We hope you like it! I wrote this last week on my eighteenth birthday!"

We were transported back to 1978 with the band. Bono's ability to put his voice through the high, open-throated ranges that made up the main melodies of this song stood strong even after all these years. He sounded remarkably like the kid that had performed this song at every U2 show over twenty years ago—except perhaps he sounded a little better.

He said, affecting the voice of a cocky eighteen-year-old, "I got on the train, I got on a boat, with my fifteen-year-old girlfriend Ali...with our demo...Mr. Record Company, I've got three songs to play for you!" The crowd roared as we were slammed back into this song of adolescent insecurity and existential angst with the start of Edge's guitar solo. Due to our extreme proximity, I felt like we could have been in a small nightclub in Dublin in 1981. A small part of me had always regretted being born in 1976, just forty-five days after U2 formed as Feedback in the kitchen at Larry's parents' house. I had regretted missing Red Rocks in 1983 and the Joshua Tree Tour. This one song's performance went a long way to make up for that lost time.

"Out of Control" finished strong, with the crowd cheering loudly, and the band went directly into "Sunday Bloody Sunday." The full meaning of the classic hit me in my heart for the first time ever, and I was brought back to the present reality of 2001. I felt the opening lyrics in a way that I never could have before. I never had a day where I couldn't believe the news before September 11th. Though I had appreciated "Sunday Bloody Sunday" as a great song, I had never been able to identify with the sentiment in the way that I now could.

I felt tears rising in my throat. I gazed up at Bono, standing just above us on stage. He set out shortly for the catwalk again. A group of people just outside the heart on Edge's side was waving the American flag in time to the beat, above their heads. Bono motioned to them to pass him the flag. He got the flag on the stage and cradled it to himself like a baby as I wiped my tears away.

I was losing myself again in this show. I was swept up from the moment they played "New Year's Day." "Stuck In A Moment" was next as Bono returned to his main post before us. This was another emotional song for America right now. We were stuck. However, I could feel myself getting unstuck, as the U2 show pulled me out of my pain. Then "Kite," and Bono could be seen from this close perspective weeping openly. His father had died since we'd seen him last. The singer's voice shook with emotion. I felt sad for him, wanted to just gather him up. The tears started up for me too, once again.

I don't know if the tears ever stopped during the show. I wasn't aware of it beyond that point because throughout the rest of this show, for a full ninety minutes, I felt as if I had been released from myself—I was gone again. Swept up in the music, the show. Gone into satori. Ironically, they didn't play "Gone" that night. Go figure.

"Angel of Harlem" was next, and Bono announced that it was dedicated to New York City. The crowd of Baltimoreans cheered at the sentiment. We sang along with Bono as best we could.

Crowd participation continued into the next song. Bono and Edge took up a notch by inviting a male fan on stage. Bono pulled him up from outside the heart and showed the crowd a sign, upon which the fan had written simply, "Knockin' on Heaven's Door" and listed the chords necessary to play the song. When the fan climbed onstage Bono told him, "I hope you can deliver!" They went into the song, and the fan did a great job. Bono gave the fan the microphone at one point, and he sang through a couple of lines with a strong lovely voice. Bono was inspired and began an improvised bit of rap about our new guitarist:

"Somewhere out of the crowd,

A man says, I wanna be a star!

You need Faith and a lot of Attitude

These two things you need if you wanna get that far

But there's no other kind of faith, brother

As the faith we have in each other..."

The acoustic set continued at the tip of the heart. I had moved out from the front by then to enjoy wider open spaces in the back of the heart, and to give some people behind me a chance to see Bono's dental work from the ultra-close vantage point I had inhabited up front. It was around this time that I looked to my left and spotted none other than Christian, my European buddy from the first leg, standing in his old spot at the back of the heart, watching the show. This was the last place I had seen him: in the same spot when U2's stage was set up in Philadelphia, and I patted him on the shoulder. We hugged, and tried to talk a little, but didn't want to miss the show so we zipped it shortly.

A song I didn't recognize at first had begun. Bono told us it was "a song about political fanatics, religious lunatics." He went on, "I'm always amazed when we see how man can remake God in his own image. I'm always amazed at how a man wants to shrink God to his own size: petty, tiny, greedy. Well, this is for... you know who this is for." The crowd cheered, agreeing.

He continued, "God is love, that's what God is." Amen, brother, I thought to myself.

"We haven't played this song in a long time. So, hush now, hush now," he said to the screaming crowd. We hushed.

"Please" was a desperate plea for peace, tinged with anger and hurt. The audience was captivated from the opening stanza. "Streets" rose into the air after the climactic end of "Please," in the perfect red transition that I had so loved during the PopMart tour. Bono read out his psalm, and the music lifted off as the audience shouted and hooted with delight and joy. It was perhaps the first bit of joy that had entered many of our lives since 9/11. The emotional response was rapturous, ecstatic. When the lights came up around the arena, I saw people all around me dancing, shouting, singing, and laughing. I hugged Ro, long and hard, and wept with joy. I grabbed him by the shoulders and hopped about madly, dragging him with me. He laughed at my childlike enthusiasm.

Things had been so bad after 9/11, I hadn't known if we would ever laugh and celebrate again. It was a tremendous relief to feel good again, to feel joy again. "I Still Haven't Found What I'm Looking For" followed, and we participated in a huge sing along. Bono lifted his arms above his head during the song's bridge, clapping and saying, "Take it to the church now!" The audience clapped along to the beat, thousands of hands in unison, and the spirit of the place soared. God had entered the building.

"Pride" capped off the end of the first set. God stayed awhile, and we felt the love as we lustily joined Bono for the classic chorus of the song. I could almost see that love, flying about the arena, as Bono shouted out "Love!" and clapped his fist to his chest then pulled his hand back and released an imaginary throw out to us. The audience returned the love throwing gesture in time to the beat of "Pride." Love bounced around the arena as we threw it back and forth to each other. As the song ended, and U2 left the stage, grins were everywhere, and the hoots and screams must have followed them backstage. Then, out of the voices of the melee, spontaneously came a distinct chorus of "Oh oh, oh oh's" to complete "Pride" as we awaited the band's return.

"Bullet" started the encore as it had in the spring, but the message to America about gun violence had been deleted. Considering current events, it really wouldn't have felt relevant. Instead, Bono led the crowd through another synchronized clapping sequence, and chanted over the ending guitar solo. "Bullet" seemed shortened a bit from the first leg, and U2 used this time to allow Bono to sing bits of "What's Going On," which had recently been remade with a coalition of artists including Bono. While "Bullet" had felt unfocused tonight, "What's Going On" hit the mark.

"New York" reappeared then, having been moved to a new spot during the encore. Bono had further changed the lyrics, and tonight he sang, "Come September, a lot can change. Summer's love turns to winter's pain, in New York. Even Baltimore loves New York." The crowd cheered at these words. As the song neared its end and Larry, Edge, and Adam took over with a rising climax of music, Bono led the crowd in a chorus of "I love NEW York! I love NEW York!" During the break before the next song, a chant rose in the audience, "USA!... USA!... USA!" I had never felt such a spirit of patriotism. Bono told us again, "I want you to know that this group would not want to be anywhere else right now. We're deeply humbled and deeply honored to be on tour in the United States of America right now." He shared with us what it was like to live in Ireland in the seventies and eighties, when the IRA was bombing Britain. He shared how some of his friends and family knew people who had been "beaten within an inch of their lives just because they spoke with an Irish accent," even though they had nothing to do with the IRA. He then spoke about the beauty of the Koran.

This was obviously a message of non-violence toward Muslims in America, and I think that many, if not most of us at the concert got it. Bono often turns people off U2 with the volume of messages that are interlaced with much of their work. Tonight, we needed these messages of hope, tolerance, and peace. We welcomed them.

"One" began as a tribute to the victims of 9/11. Hundreds of names scrolled past on blue screens behind the band. Every name marked an American life taken on that horrible day, and I knew I wasn't the only one crying in the arena this time.

And finally, seamlessly, "Walk On" began. It marked the end of this night of healing. Bono shouted out "USA!" at the top of the song, and it became an anthem of courage for us tonight. "Be strong!" he shouted out to us as U2 prepared to leave the stage. The song challenged us to leave it behind; leave the pain behind, leave the anger and resentment behind as best we could, even for this incredible hurt, so that we could move forward together toward brighter tomorrows. The lights came up again when U2 left the stage and we all regarded each other one last time, glowing with renewal.

After U2 exited, I found Christian still standing near me, and we discussed further tour plans. He was surprised to learn that I wasn't going to the upcoming show in Philly, and that in fact I would only catch one more show, in Denver on November 7th. When I told him that Ro and I would have reserved seats in Denver, he shrugged it off, saying, "Ah, we'll get you down here [into the heart]." We exchanged cell phone numbers and email addresses and planned to meet up in Denver before the show. As Ro and I departed the arena to head back to his vehicle, I watched the crowds dissipating. Smiles were everywhere. Most were as large as mine.

What happened in Baltimore that night was happening around the country at every U2 show that fall. U2 was spreading healing. America had already fallen in love with U2 again after the first leg of the Elevation Tour. The events of September 11th had added a dimension to their success; that is, U2 was relevant again, and perhaps more relevant to Americans than they had ever been before. In the autumn of 2001, a little U2 went a long way in helping us to move on past the devastation of 9/11.

I spent the three weeks following the Baltimore show planning for a five-day visit to Denver around the weekend of my twenty-fifth birthday and the show scheduled at Denver's Pepsi Center for Wednesday, November 7th. This would be my last stop on the Elevation Tour. Part of the reason that I hadn't attempted to get General Admission tickets was that I wouldn't have the time to sit in line all day. Most of the time in Denver would be spent looking at apartments and doing job interviews, in anticipation of our move, slated to happen in less than two months. My priorities were changing as the tour ended for me and a new world opened with the idea of starting fresh, beginning again, in a new location and a much-needed change from Northern Virginia which had served as my home ground since I was twelve years old.

Denver felt great when I arrived there on Monday, November 5th. My brother Mike, who had made the city his family's home since the early nineties, picked me up at the bus stop from Denver International Airport. I hadn't been in Colorado since the summer of 1992, at age fifteen, when I had first fallen in love with the Rockies as I anticipated my first U2 concert later that very summer.

Denver was cool! I liked it right away and even more so the next day when Mike took me downtown for a day of looking at apartments. The city felt right to me as Mike pointed at various landmarks and tried to help orient me. I loved the inexpensive apartments that I saw in the Capitol Hill area. I felt my plans becoming more real.

On Wednesday November 7th, Ro joined me in Denver. We would be staying with my friend Alie from college, who had made Colorado her home a year prior. I picked up a rental car and headed back out to the airport to meet Ro, then we found our way to Alie's home.

A few hours later, after catching up at Alie's house, the three of us headed out the door towards downtown. My sense of respect for the city increased as we rode through busy streets and I gazed at skyscrapers looming above, seeing them lit up in the night for the first time. Christian and I had been in communication since the Baltimore show, and we headed down towards Coors Field first to find my tour compadre at a nearby Irish pub that was hosting a pre-concert party.

After a little minor difficulty, we found the bar and Christian, who introduced us to some of his U2-ey friends. They didn't come into the bar with us because they were off to the venue a little early. Christian joined Alie, Ro, and me in the pub for a few pints of Guinness, and I was glad to be able to hang with him a little while. I didn't know if I'd ever see him again after tonight.

Because of that, the pub time was tinged with a little sadness for me. I regretted that I wouldn't have the opportunity to get to know Christian better. I had come to think of him as a friend and felt that we had been through the tour together. We had shared the excitement back in May, the disappointment in July, and now the renewal in these fall shows.

The bar was loud and brimming with U2 fans, U2 music, and U2 videos on a big screen TV. It was quite a scene and we sat and tried to talk over the party and a few beers with some so-called traditional Irish food. As usual, I was too excited to eat, so I supped on more than one Guinness while I awaited my final U2 show of the year.

I was a little drunk as the four of us headed back to Alie's car. I hadn't forgotten Christian's promise to get us down into the heart tonight. We discussed the battle plan on the way to the venue. Ro wasn't too pressed about getting into the heart again, but he was up for whatever in his easy, laid-back fashion. Alie was cool either way too, though she had reportedly been a bit of a U2 fanatic herself in the years before we had met at college in the mid-90s. She was eager to get her first close-up view of the band.

We arrived on the scene and found a parking spot at around 7:00 PM. The opening band, No Doubt, would be taking the stage before too long. Christian went in the general admission door and said he would meet us at the entrance to a reserved seating section in the 200-level. Ro and Alie and I went upstairs to find bathrooms and beer. It was hectic in the halls of the arena, with excited people flying every which way. Merchandise racks were set up all over and Jubilee tables were pitched, with banners hanging from them. Young people collected signatures for a petition to George Bush telling him to drop the debt, and they encouraged fans to take postcards with the White House's mailing address on them, to snail mail a note to the president later.

Christian found me then at the meeting point. He told me what the wristband combination on the floor was tonight and reported that he had only one of each. I looked through my collection and found two more of each—what luck! Alie and Ro said they were going to go check out our reserved seats and then would meet up with us in the heart later. They left with the recycled wristbands in their pockets and some scotch tape. I taped mine on to match Christian's, and we headed down into the heart with no problem.

Once safely inside, I looked around over my beer at the familiar scene for one last time. Christian said Mike was up front that night, in the tightly packed cluster that surrounded Bono's main stage position. We stood back in the relaxed rear portion of the giant heart and watched the scene while we chatted. Friends were everywhere. People I had met along the way, and people I had never met but recognized from the previous shows. I spotted Otto Kitsinger and reintroduced myself to him. I hadn't contacted him since our meeting at the Baltimore show, and he reported he'd been on the road with the tour, and offline anyway. He would be going to the show in Salt Lake City in two days and asked why I wasn't going, especially being that it was going to be on my birthday! That was okay, I told him, I would be celebrating tonight and that was enough.

Tonight was also the four-year mark since the St. Louis show when I was pulled up to hug Bono at length on-stage. I was happier tonight to be quietly in the crowd, amongst friends. You see, it wasn't just about the band tonight for me. It was about saying goodbye to this phenomenal group of people, this community that I had come home to. This would be my last tour night to spend with them for at least a few years, if not longer.

No Doubt was the opener tonight, and I admired Gwen Stefani's high-energy stage performance. The band rocked hard enough to get the Denver crowd going strong. After No Doubt's too short set, Ro and Alie joined me in the heart. Alie was quite excited to be so close to the stage, and we waited for the show to start together. I left to go to the bathroom before U2 came on and picked up a couple more beers. I was surprised on the way back in to have my wristband tugged on by security. It seemed they were copping on to what was happening in the heart as more and more fans were being smuggled in from the seats. It was very crowded that night, more crowded than I had ever seen before.

Shortly after I, luckily, made it back into the heart, U2 took the stage. The crowd was rocking from the first moment. I screamed with everyone and sucked on another beer as I watched, trying to get the drink down so I could jump with everybody else.

Then, we were off! It was one last ride on this Elevation plane for Marcy. Bono remarked early on about the literal elevation of tonight's locale: Denver, of course, being the Mile-High City. During "Beautiful Day," Ro tapped me on the shoulder and said, "Look!", pointing to my left side. I turned and was surprised to see Gwen Stefani immediately to my left, flanked by her bandmates as they all rocked out watching the show. I tried not to stare and laughed as a guy standing in front of Gwen turned quickly to take a picture of his friend who had snuck up next to her and pretended to put his arm around her. Gwen didn't seem to notice as the guy slipped away. She just kept rocking.

I turned from that scene and my attention went back to Bono and the band. The show went on in much the same fashion as it had in Baltimore a few weeks ago. We were treated to "Out of Control" again, and this time a male fan guitarist was pulled up onstage to play "All Along the Watchtower," a song I had never heard the band play in concert. The show continued through the next hour or so; then came the encore.

The band started playing "Walk On." This was it for me, and out came the waterworks as I felt my heart cracking open and wanting to turn back time on the end of this tour. I took strength in the message of the title of this song. It was over, this made it official. The large quantity of beers that I had consumed made me even more emotional than usual, and I watched the performance through a flood of tears, feeling broken-hearted. I took in the scene one last time in this context. I would never experience Elevation again.

As Bono sang the final lines of the song, the drumbeat rose with the lights that lit the arena with the lyrics to the song's coda. I smiled through my tears as Bono said goodbye and thank you once again. I knew I was gonna miss seeing them, although a big part of me was ready to leave the show behind.

The Hallelujah chorus echoed through the arena, and I strained on my tiptoes to see the band, see Bono, Edge, Adam, and Larry wave goodbye until next time. The audience cheered them as they went on their way, leaving the stage, and leaving most of our lives until the next tour. I looked around as the house lights came up. I wiped the tears off my face, though I couldn't hide my puffy, watery eyes. Christian was to my left and I turned and hugged him and gave him my collection of wristbands for his further adventures. He would be seeing a fair few more shows before the tour's end in early December and might be able to use them. "Are you sure?" he said as I nodded and told him to have a great time at the rest of the shows. I spotted Mike then and ran over to embrace him. My tears started fresh. This fan friend I had been in communication with since last February.

We disentangled as I had to run to catch up with Alie and Ro.

My tears betrayed a lingering reluctance to leave.

"I'll see you on the next tour!" Mike called out sweetly after me as I exited the heart.

EPILOGUE:
ON TO THE MIRACLE

On June 6, 2015, I woke groggy and sleepy eyed with a sore head. Morning was breaking on the day of the first Innocence and Experience show in Denver, Colorado. The night before, I had been at a spirited celebration in the Hard Rock Cafe where Denver's beloved tribute band Under a Blood Red Sky had performed for the many U2 diehards in the city. We had celebrated in anticipation of two U2 concerts scheduled in our hometown over the weekend.

    I rose quickly and got dressed in excitement for the day. The velvet dress I donned was a nod to that moment nearly eighteen years ago when I had met Bono on stage in St. Louis. I was hoping to meet him again today, amongst friends who felt more like family. We would wait together for the band's arrival to the Pepsi Center. I had something in mind to give to Bono.

My fourteen-month-old daughter would stay home with a hired nanny today while I went off on this adventure. I had splurged at great expense and found an appropriate caregiver for her so that I wouldn't miss any of this weekend's celebrations. I kissed my cutie goodbye and got into my car where I took long pulls off my vape pen and relaxed as the THC took away my hangover. I kept some edibles tucked in my bag, to keep my buzz going through the long day ahead.

At the second flower shop where I stopped, I found irises. The "Songs of Innocence" album had been released in 2014, the year I had become a mother. What beautiful synchronicity, to get to know the song about Bono's mother Iris the same year my child was born.

On the light rail I sat solo, holding the flowers in the lap of my burgundy velvet dress. My U2OPIA license plate was in my bag, and it was early in the day. I was heading to the Pepsi Center stop to meet Elsha Stockseth and her family who had traveled from out of state, to wait with them for the band's arrival.

Once on scene at the arena, I was reunited with Elsha and her parents. To my delight, Billy Bunting turned up too. Billy had become like a big brother to me over the course of the last number of years. I followed his U2 tribute band Under a Blood Red Sky with a tenacity that mirrored my former stubbornness about following the real thing. It was easy to love Billy, and it was easy to be loved by him too. He was a deep well of generosity and natural warmth, and he channeled the spirit of U2 faithfully for the local U2 family.

Billy came bearing a gift for Bono that day too. Billy carried an original photo of Bono performing at Red Rocks in 1983, taken by local photographer Greg Wigler, whom I had met years prior at a UABRS gig. The few of us early comers found a curb near the entrance where it was believed the band would arrive within the next several hours. Suddenly, the sky opened, and a dramatic early summer downpour had us running for cover. We waited for it to clear under a small nook at the outside corner of the arena, and companionably discussed the gifts and items we had brought to share with the band, should they stop and chat today.

Billy was looking fantastic in his jacket modeled after the one Bono had worn on the Elevation tour, complete with American flag lining. He chuckled with me over my choice of apparel. As always, I was delighted to be in Billy's company. He had sung his heart out the night before, as he always did. To me he was a rock star.

The rain cleared, so we resumed waiting at our spot on the curb near the entrance to the restricted area. More fans were joining, and the line stretched out to our left and right. Many familiar faces appeared. The fan community was live and online throughout this tour. We were connected in real time to a degree we never had been before.

Crisp memories from the day arise out of the marijuana-induced haze that was my perspective. The first band member to show up was the elusive Larry. He walked toward the line waving as we cheered. He started near our end of the lineup, signing, and moving down the row of fans. The fans were directed to stay on the curb as Larry walked down the road, there was no additional barrier between us. Some autograph hounds had turned up and pushed their items towards Larry from behind me. He looked up at them with a clear flare of irritation and snapped, "Really?!" He shook his head and stepped around Elsha's wheelchair just to my right as he greeted her with a smile. I let him pass without saying a word because I was confused about his flare of irritation, and a little intimidated.

"What just happened?" I whispered to my friend Melody, who stood to my left. She wasn't sure either, and we kept on watching and waiting to see what was next. Larry continued down the growing line. I spied happily from a bit of a distance as our friend Deena presented him with her book <u>On the Road with U2: My Musical Journey</u>, and Larry hugged her! I felt her joy. Larry was her favorite, and after all these years, maybe she was his too!

The sun began to break through the clouds and before long The Edge had arrived. I was buzzing quite strongly by then, both from the adrenaline of these encounters, and from the marijuana edibles I had consumed as we waited there. Edge walked the line, not signing today, but sharing the twinkle in his eyes as he shook hands. The ground was still wet from the downpour, and the sunlight sparkled and warmed us as Edge came through, shaking Melody's hand, and mine. By this time my license plate was hanging from a shoestring around my neck, and he glanced at it, raising an eyebrow as he smiled at me. I laughed and looked away, suddenly feeling shy. He stopped to my right, chatting with Elsha and her family as I recovered from the moment of eye contact and wordless communication with The Edge.

The scene was growing busier as 3:00 PM came and went. The line of waiting fans stretched all the way down the curb, and more and more of us took place at the end of the line. The energy grew as we continued to wait for a chance to greet Bono.

My dear friend Heather joined me in waiting. She promised to take a photo if the moment came that I would give to the irises to Bono. I had been emboldened to move into this action by something that had happened at the shows in Phoenix two weekends prior. My friend Caryn and I had found ourselves there in possession of two incredible reserved seats: fifth row aisle, just on Adam's side of the main stage. During the opening song, I had held up my U2OPIA license plate and waved it at Bono as he sauntered over toward our spot, singing "The Miracle." He had stopped a moment, studied the plate, and then unmistakably pointed at me as I held it high.

Zoom! I was off to the races once again... what a hit!

So here I stood, two weeks later, stoned and slightly self-conscious, but mostly filled with an overflowing love and gratitude for the continued presence, support, and inspiration of U2 music, U2 concerts, and U2 community in my life. I was ready to step forward and give something back, ready to be seen again. The irises had been wrapped with their stems in water, so they remained fresh, and some of them were yet to open. I could feel good to give them to Bono today, should I be so blessed to have this chance.

Sometime after 3:00 PM, the large black vehicle serving as Bono's transport stopped at the far end of the line. He disembarked to begin a very slow walk, greeting the dozens of fans waiting for him. He moved slowly, mindfully, down the line. He was laughing, chatting, and hugging fans as they presented themselves to him. I was beside myself with excitement and nerves. Luckily Heather was beside me too, reminding me to breathe as we waited about thirty minutes for him to reach us.

He came to Billy first. Billy reached out his hand from the second row on the curb and introduced himself humbly as the singer in the local U2 tribute band. Hearing this, Bono kept Billy's hand clasped in his own and pulled him forth from the curb to stand next to him in the road for a talk. I was blessed to witness these two beautiful rays of light communing like old friends for the next several minutes.

Bono placed his arm around Billy's shoulder companionably as Billy showed the star his mirrored U2 fly shades, and the photo from Red Rocks. Bono good naturedly declined the offer of taking the shades to wear onstage tonight, chuckling as he remarked, "I think I'd get into trouble if I did that!" He accepted the photo taken by Greg Wigler at Red Rocks in 1983, saying he had never seen this one before. Billy spoke to Bono about the show UABRS had played at Red Rocks some years back, and Bono said he had heard about it. Amazing!

Soon the two of them shook hands and Billy stepped back into the line. As Bono's gaze turned to the remainder of the fans, I fell back on an old line that had served me well when I had greeted him seventeen years before: "Bono, can I give you something?"

He stepped towards me, "Sure!"

I presented the irises to him, and he took them, appearing delighted, "They're beautiful!"

He smiled and leaned in towards me. My arms were already wide open to receive him, and I wrapped him in a giant bear hug. I said softly to him, "Thank you for sharing her with us," referring to his mother Iris, whose spirit was gifted to all of us when Bono wrote the words to the song that was named after her.

The photo that Heather snapped as she stood just behind me in that moment reveals a gently smiling Bono leaning towards me as I hug him, and Brian Murphy the bodyguard smiling in the background. As Bono stepped back and moved on to Elsha, he pointed at my license plate and said something, but I was so overwhelmed that I didn't catch his words, so I just nodded and laughed weakly. Once again, my mind was blown, and I faded back into the crowd.

Heather showed me the photo. It was beautiful. My heart felt as if it was growing bigger than my body. She posted it to Facebook, captioned "Bono love!" Was that what this was?

I looked and there was our friend Melody, and we all moved together towards the neighboring bar. I needed a drink! Billy was nowhere to be found now.

In Brooklyn's, I changed out of the velvet dress and into a concert T-shirt. I found more local U2 friends at the bar and proceeded to celebrate with shots.

Later, inside the arena, I found Billy near the rail at the e-stage and hugged him for a photo. I pulled deeply on my vape pen as I waited behind one person at the rail near the e-stage for the show to begin. I remember very little of the show that night.

The next morning, I woke with a pounding head and grabbed my phone. Our friend Jen had tagged me and Billy in a post to Facebook, "OMG! Billy Bunting and Marcy Gannon, Bono Instagrammed your gifts!"

As soon as I could figure out what that meant, I signed up to Instagram. The newest post on U2's page was a photo of the irises, buds opening in the image, next to Billy's gift, captioned:

Something to read, something to smell—Bono

That night at Denver's second show, my daughter was asleep in her carrier, heavy on my chest as Bono and Edge performed a version of Paul Simon's "Mother and Child Reunion." I looked down at her with so much love as the lights rose and the introduction to "Streets" took over. The crowd's cheers grew in joyful volume as I said a quiet prayer of thanks for her, and for the music that had brought her to me. If there were no U2 music, she wouldn't have been at all.

You see, I came to know my only child's father while he played guitar as The Edge in Billy's tribute band, Under A Blood Red Sky. Through these connections, this little one became my miracle. On June 7, 2015, as we left the arena amongst throngs of happy fans, she woke smiling with a magical post-show glow. We were innocence and experience, happy to be heading home together.

Sometimes, she still speaks to me in U2 lyrics. As U2 always did, she gives me hope.

A LETTER TO YOU FROM THE AUTHOR

August 2021

Dearest Beautiful Reader,

Twenty years have passed since the happenings from the Elevation Tour that are described in this little memoir. So why did I wait so long to publish?

I got lost for a while. As you may have noticed, there was a lot of drinking going on, and beer was a constant companion through many of these stories. In the years that followed, my drinking was mitigated by my preferred drug, marijuana.

After I burned out my U2 addiction in 2001, I got focused on getting high. My focus remained there through three more U2 tours, continuing through late 2015, when I finally found a bottom and my feet were set upon a rock.

U2 music was the earliest form of a drug to which I had reliable access. After the Elevation Tour, when U2 music no longer got me high as it once did, the drinking and weed smoking ramped up and up. Things became hazy. Hence, it would be difficult, if not impossible, for me to share in such detail the few adventures I had on the Vertigo tour, the many shows I attended on the 360 Tours, and the handful I saw during the Innocence Tour. I simply wasn't writing coherently, nor was I retaining memories.

The band remained somewhat accessible to the fans during subsequent tours, as they had been on the Elevation Tour. However, until 2011, I avoided coming eye-to-eye with the band members. I had gone through the roller coaster ride of in-your-face fandom, and I didn't want to annoy any of them any further.

For more than a decade, parts of me genuinely regretted my behavior on the first leg of the tour in 2001. I felt ashamed. This self-shaming was a pattern I lived by, and my recovery teacher says that shame is the root of all addiction.

Although I went to some effort in late 2002 to find a publisher for this work, before long, my interest fell away, and I believe that was partly due to shame as well.

I'm not ashamed anymore.

This is my story.

Today, in August 2021, we find ourselves again in a post 9/11 energy. The pandemic is not over. We are still waiting for our release, our Baltimore show. We wait to dance to "Streets" together. We wait for the lights to flash on again. Some of us wonder if they ever will.

Right now, as I write this letter to you, I am working as a nurse inside a COVID-19 mass vaccination clinic. This is our new normal…and there is hope here. I release this record of events now because I am hopeful that a U2 fan out there may catch a hint of the joy of being at a U2 show; that the wait for the return of the red rising lights may be made easier as they turn these pages. If that U2 fan is you, I love you.

Going through this book again after so many years has sparked a much-needed lightness in my own heart. It has filled my spirit with joy as I revisit these shows, one by one, and all the kindred spirits with whom I was privileged to dance along the way. Maybe you were one of them, and you'll write to me and tell me about it.

I am grateful for my sobriety today, that I can open up this old project, dust it off, shine it up a bit, and offer it to you if you will have it.

And I am grateful for you.

With So Much Love,

Marcy

P.S. An Invitation

The fact that you are still here makes you one of the kindred. I know a resonance with you, even though we've likely never met. You are one of my energetic kind.

These days, along with being a nurse, I am a Holistic Wellness Coach. As such, I have a few questions to set before you with love:

What did you get from reading this story?

What major life journey did you learn from, and what did you learn from taking your journey?

What journey is calling to you *now*?

What do you imagine you could learn when you embark upon this journey?

Here is what I know: you have all the answers to all the questions within you. The place Beyond Elevation is where you'll find them, sitting quietly, waiting patiently for your attention to come within. Waiting for your presence to present itself. What gifts there are to be uncovered. What joy! I can see it like a soft valley, lush and green and fragrant. The way there is unlocked by the key that is your consciousness.

If you are called to explore within to find that place, I would be delighted to serve as your guide into the inside. We all hold that place within. That's where we connect. This connection is the opposite of addiction, the opposite of desire. This is true recovery. It's whole and complete within each one of us, patiently waiting to be discovered. If you are called, I would love to go there with you.

We have an adventure to take together. And I do love an adventure! You thought you were done with this story, and so did I…perhaps we've just begun.

ABOUT THE AUTHOR

Marcy Gannon is a Registered Nurse, Certified Yoga Teacher, and Board-Certified Nurse Coach who lives in Colorado with her recovery partner, her daughter, and Jeff the Cat.

You can connect with her via her Instagram account @elevationandbeyond.